horst hamann

vertical view

teNeues

A Production by EDITION**PANORAMA** Germany

horst hamann

Contents

8 Introduction

22 Verticals

152 Timeline

160 Biography

"A mind that is stretched to a new idea never returns to it's original dimension."

Oliver Wendell Holmes

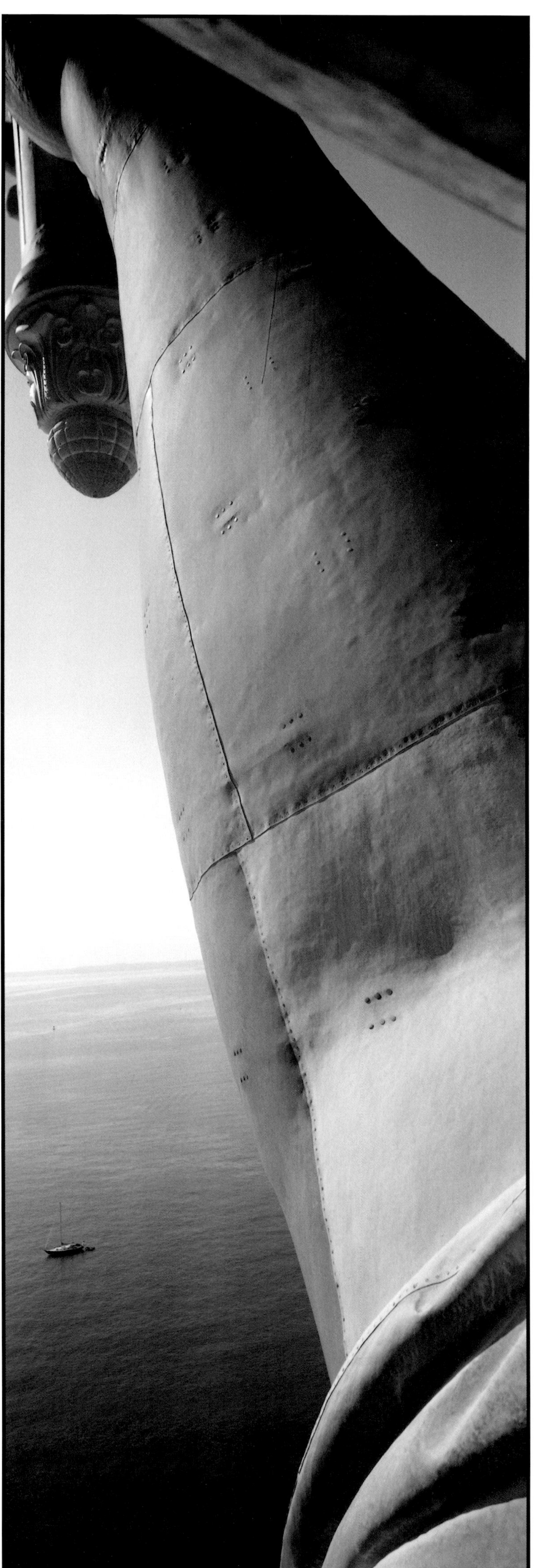

Statue of Liberty, Detail, New York 1996

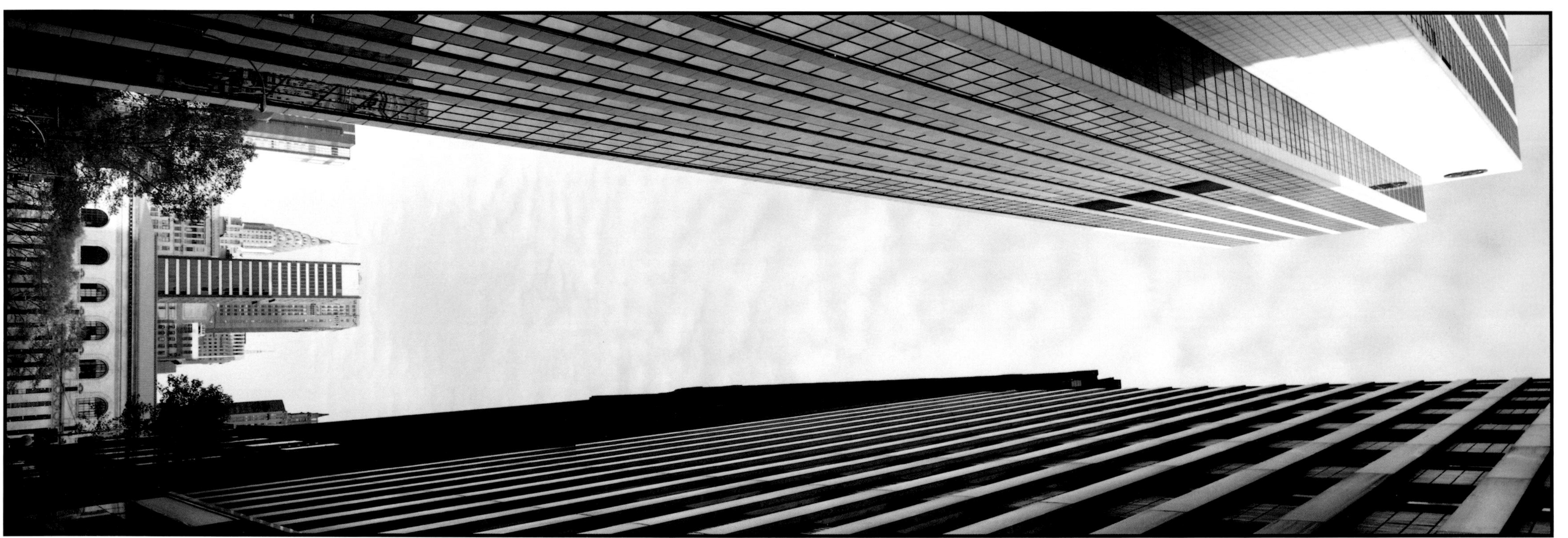

Bryant Park, 41st Street, New York 1991

Pictures, or so the saying goes, are like windows through which you can look at a unique and often strange world. Good pictures, so the saying continues, not only offer a view of a different reality, but even enable us to access great spatial depth or extensive landscape panoramas. In other words, if one of these successful vistas or insights tempts us to such an extent that we want to completely immerse ourselves in it and briefly leave our real world, then we endeavor to find a way of penetrating the idiosyncratic world of the picture. So let us imagine we enter them like burglars or secret lovers - cautiously and carefully - by climbing some imaginary ladder, slipping through this tempting window, into the space offered behind. The very moment we smoothly swing our feet over the window sill and cross the threshold between here and there, we lose sight of the artwork's frame. We are in the picture. Once we have thus changed sides we can forget for a while where it was we came from and can completely submerge ourselves in the artificial world which has now become real for us. However, as a rule we cannot tarry there for long. For even the most artful of constructs is too unstable. Sooner or later reality reins us back in. We climb back through the window which had only a few moments before been our point of entry. And, with our re-emergence in the old reality, the frame disappears once again.

If customary pictures function like windows, then Horst Hamann's „Vertical Views" can analogously be compared with narrow, high doors. Some of these doors appear to open outwards, while others evidently open inwards. Some of them are only just ajar. We approach them hesitantly. Yet most of them seem very inviting, like wide open, permeable lock gates that suck us in almost without us noticing the fact. And they attract not only our gaze, but us as physical viewers, as vertical beings. Horst Hamann's pictures do not require us to climb up and squeeze through some narrow visual or intellectual gap to get in. The impressive thing about these portrait format photographs is their openness and accessibility. This property stems from the use of the simple and in a sense almost formalist use of a classical panorama camera panning not horizontally but vertically. This straightforward, yet pioneering pan, and its effect is decidedly surprising, turns the window into a door.

It is hard to say what use we can make in our everyday lives of the experiences kindled by the picture. We can probably hardly bring anything to bear directly. Yet most of those who have completely immersed themselves in Horst Hamann's vertical views will see a walk through the streets of New York, Hong Kong or Paris through different eyes, experience it with different feelings and expectations. It may also be that in future they will never again be indifferent as to the format of a photograph. For they have witnessed how simple it is to be in the picture and that you do not necessarily need a ladder or some other means of assistance.

The key experiment which enabled Hamann to achieve this shift in paradigm took place in Bryant Park on New York's 41st Street in 1991. There, using a Linhof panorama camera he initially produced quite conventional and not utterly satisfactory horizontal photographs, with the metropolis' skyline in the background. All these photos had a sense of the limited view of reality afforded by the slit in a tank's turret. When Hamann went back to the same place and turned the camera 90 degrees for the sake of curiosity and simply because he liked experimenting, the results were striking: pictures which, in direct comparison with the horizontal counterparts, showed the same surroundings in a quite stunningly different way. Suddenly, the cityscape opens out before our eyes, while it had previously laid like a heavy bolt slotted into place across the photograph. While the landscape format made the skyline seem a long way off and made it hard to access the picture, the portrait format minimizes the distance between photograph and viewer.

However decisive the change in perspective from horizontal to vertical is, it does not in itself explain the appeal of Horst Hamann's photographs. Needless to say, the distribution of light, the emphatic sculpting of light and dark, the careful choice of grey tones all play a crucial role. In his vertical b&tw photos, Hamann likewise relies on almost classical values such as structure, composition, balance, density and refinement. Irrespective of the format (which precisely in this case cannot be completely separated from the contents), the pictures can be described not only as open doors, but also, for want of a better term, as ingeniously expansive, highly charged surfaces. As surfaces on which the objective, visible form collides with a subjective, personal view, whereby in the most successful of these works the collision strikes a resounding vibrant note. In concrete terms, this means that the print of a street in New York presented in the frame and behind the glass can be understood as the afore-mentioned expansive and highly charged surface. Like some taut tympanum it remains mute until the committed gaze of the observer sets it vibrating.

It is striking just how many of Hamann's photographs, for all their expansive all-over compositions, also hinge on drawing our gaze into the distance. Indeed, at times you get the impression that this gaze into open space is a basic unobtrusive feature of all these pictures. Even the depiction of a basketball player - it fills the entire frame - is linked before our inner eye with the notion of free movement in a wide expanse. In other words, Horst Hamann not only involves the viewer in terms of his or her entire body, complete with skin and hair, he also gives the viewer sufficient scope in the photographs to feel free and easy rather than constrained and ensnared.

In the final instance, the stimulating attraction of these photographs stems from the interplay of different states and things. Hamann's pictures are all the more important, the greater the freedom accorded them to leave the relationship of definition and openness itself undecided.

If a photograph is successful, then photographer and viewer share the joy that this creates. The photographer is satisfied and the viewer is grateful - two sides of one and the same coin. For the photographer is grateful to possess the talent and unknown vigour which enables him to create the picture. And the viewer is grateful to encounter a work which satisfies his or her desires. All visually-minded persons have sensed this at some point and been enriched in the course of their lives by a few good pictures. Poor pictures should be forgotten as quickly as possible. Although, as with a good wine, it is not easy to describe what goes to make up a good picture. You cannot measure, weigh up or count the properties required to create the best of the Bordeauxs. In the final analysis, there is only one way to analyze the quality - namely to try a drop, to try another drop, and so on. And the same applies to pictures. Only by looking at many pictures, be practising comparative vision, can you enhance your enjoyment and the insights you gain. It goes without saying, you have to talk about the good pictures and your experience of them, need to tell others what you see, think, and feel. Precisely in that order. If you were only to see, or to think, or to feel, you would not get very far. Vladimir Nabokov repeatedly recommended that a good book should not just be read with the heart. The heart is a remarkably stupid reader, so he suggested. That said, no artwork should be approached solely by means of the brain - but instead using both the brain and the spine. In truth, the tingling along our spines tells us what the photographer felt when taking a great photo and wanted to have us feel. It hardly bears stating that the spine runs vertically.

Andreas Bee
(Museum für Moderne Kunst, Frankfurt/Main)

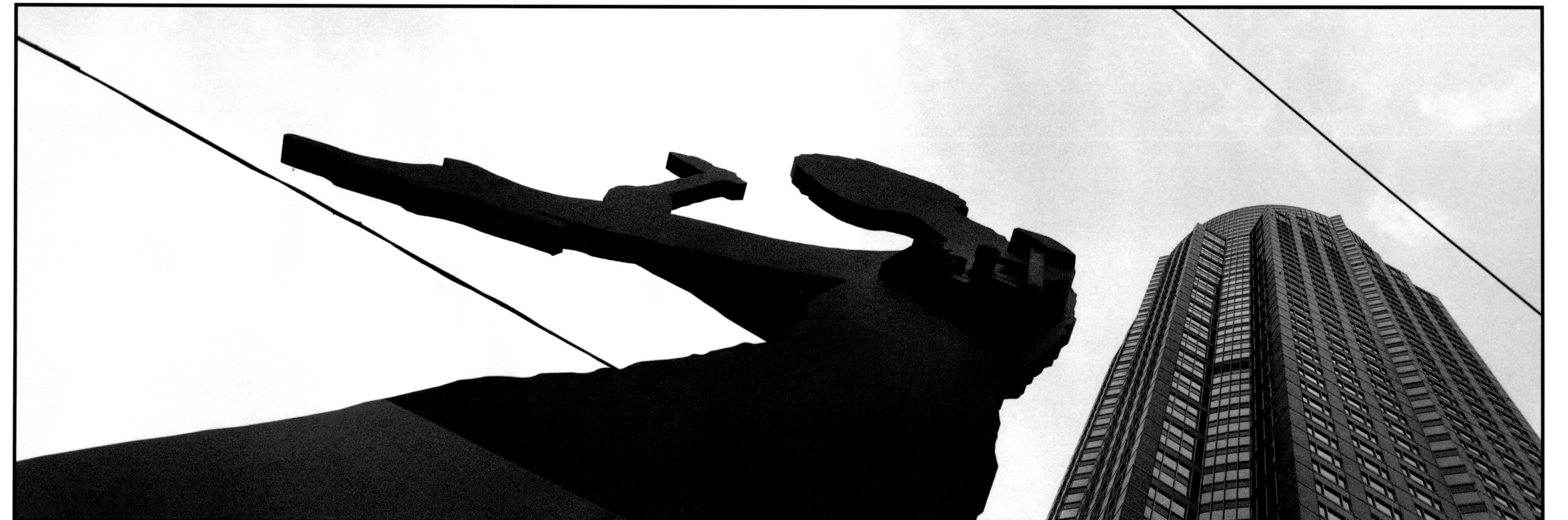

The Hammering Man, Frankfurt / Main 1999

Bilder, sagt man, seien wie Fenster, durch die man in eine eigene, oft fremdartig anmutende Welt schauen könne. Gute Bilder heißt es weiter, geben nicht nur den Blick auf eine andere Wirklichkeit frei, sondern sie ermöglichen sogar den Zugang zu tiefen Raumfluchten und ausgedehnten Landschaftspanoramen. Lockt uns also einer dieser gelungenen Aus- oder Einblicke derart, daß wir Lust bekommen, ganz darauf einzugehen und unsere reale Welt für kurze Zeit zu verlassen, so müssen wir uns bemühen, einen Weg zu finden, wie wir in die eigentümliche Welt des Bildes eindringen können. Stellen wir uns also vor, wir steigen wie ein Einbrecher oder heimlicher Liebhaber, vorsichtig und konzentriert, über eine imaginäre Leiter durch eines dieser verführerischen Bildfenster in den dargebotenen Raum ein. In dem Augenblick, wo wir uns geschmeidig über die Fensterbank schwingen und die Schwelle zwischen hier und dort überschreiten, verschwindet der Rahmen des Kunstwerkes aus unserem Blick. Wir sind im Bild. Haben wir erst einmal die Seiten gewechselt, können wir für eine Weile vergessen, woher wir kamen und ganz aufgehen in der künstlichen Welt, die nun für uns zur realen geworden ist. Nur lange verweilen können wir dort in der Regel nicht. Zu instabil ist noch das gelungenste Konstrukt. Früher oder später ruft uns die Realität zurück. Wir klettern abermals durch das Fenster, durch das wir vor kurzem gekommen waren. Und nun verschwindet der Rahmen mit dem Wiedereinstieg in die alte Realität zum zweiten Mal.

Wenn herkömmliche Bilder wie Fenster funktionieren, dann lassen sich die „Vertical Views" von Horst Hamann in Analogie hierzu mit schmalen und hohen Türen vergleichen. Manche dieser Türen scheinen nach außen zu schwingen, andere öffnen sich nach innen. Einige stehen nur einen Spalt breit offen. Ihnen nähert man sich zögerlich. Die meisten jedoch wirken geradezu einladend, wie weit geöffnete, durchlässige Schleusen und ziehen den Betrachter fast unmerklich in den Raum hinein. Wohlgemerkt nicht nur den Blick, sondern den Betrachter als ganzen, als vertikales Subjekt. Bei den Bildern von Horst Hamann muß sich niemand kletternd bemühen und sich durch einen schmalen visuellen oder intellektuellen Spalt Einlaß verschaffen. Das Beeindruckende an den hoch-formatigen Bildern ist ihre Offenheit und Zugänglichkeit. Diese Eigenart gründet in der so simpel und formalistisch anmutenden Drehung der klassischen Panoramakamera von der Horizontalen in die Vertikale. Durch jene einfache, aber wegweisende und in ihrer Wirkung ganz und gar über-raschende Wendung wird aus dem Fenster eine Tür.

Was sich von den im Bild gemachten Erfahrungen im Alltag verwerten läßt, ist schwer zu sagen. Im Verhältnis 1 : 1 können wir wahrscheinlich kaum etwas übertragen. Die meisten aber, die sich einmal ganz und gar auf die vertikalen Bilder von Horst Hamann eingelassen haben, werden einen Gang durch New

York, Hongkong oder Paris mit anderen Augen, Gefühlen und Erwartungen erleben. Auch könnte es sein, daß ihnen in Zukunft das Format einer Fotografie nie mehr gleichgültig ist. Denn sie haben erlebt, daß es ganz leicht sein kann, ins Bild zu gelangen, daß es dazu nicht unbedingt einer Leiter oder anderer Hilfsmittel bedarf.

Das entscheidende Experiment, mit dem Hamann der Paradigmenwechsel gelang, fand 1991 im Bryant Park an der 41st Street in New York statt. Hier entstanden mit einer Linhof-Panoramakamera zunächst recht konventionelle, nicht sehr befriedigend horizontale Fotografien mit der Skyline der Metropole im Hintergrund. Sämtliche Aufnahmen wirkten wie begrenzte Ausblicke durch den Seeschlitz eines Panzerwagens. Als Hamann aus Neugier und Freude am Experiment an gleicher Stelle die Kamera einmal um 90 Grad drehte, erhielt er plötzlich Bilder, die im direkten Vergleich mit den horizontalen Ergebnissen derselben Umgebung schockierend anders wirkten. Plötzlich öffnete sich die vordem wie ein schwerer Querriegel darliegende Stadtlandschaft dem Blick. Während noch das Querformat die Skyline weit entfernt und den Zugang zum Bildraum schwierig erscheinen ließ, verkürzte sich im Hochformat die Distanz zwischen Bild und Betrachter auf ein Minimum.

So entscheidend der Perspektivenwechsel von der Horizontalen in die Vertikale auch war, er allein erklärt die Attraktion der Bilder von Horst Hamann nicht. Natürlich spielen die Verteilung des Lichtes, die ausgeprägte Modellierung von Hell und Dunkel und die sorgfältig kalkulierten Grauwerte eine entscheidende Rolle. Auch in seinen vertikalen Schwarzweiß-Aufnahmen baut Hamann auf beinahe klassisch anmutende Werte wie Struktur, Komposition, Ausgewogenheit, Dichte und Raffinement. Unabhängig vom Format, das gerade in diesem Fall vom Inhalt nie vollkommen zu trennen ist, lassen sich die Bilder nicht nur als offene Türen, sondern versuchsweise auch als gekonnt gespannte Oberflächen beschreiben. Als Flächen, auf denen die objektive, sichtbare Form und eine subjektive, persönliche Anschauung aufeinanderstoßen und wo dieser Zusammenstoß, bei den gelungensten Werken, zu nachhaltig klingenden Schwingungen führt. Konkret bedeutet dies, daß der im Rahmen hinter Glas präsentierte Abzug einer Straßenschlucht in New York beispielsweise als die beschriebene Spannungsfläche zu verstehen wäre. Diese bleibt, vergleichbar einem straff aufgezogenen Trommelfell, solange stumm, bis sie durch das Engagement des Betrachters in Schwingung versetzt wird.

Auffällig ist, wie viele Fotografien von Hamann trotz formatfüllender Kompositionen den Blick in die Ferne mit einbeziehen. Streckenweise gewinnt man sogar den Eindruck, als sei dieser Blick in den offenen Raum ein unaufdringlicher, aber allen Bildern innewohnender Grundakkord. Selbst noch die Darstellung eines rahmenfüllenden Basketballspielers verbindet sich vor dem inneren Auge mit der Vorstellung von freier Bewegung in weitem Raum. Horst Hamann bezieht also nicht nur den Betrachter mit dem ganzen Körper, mit Haut und Haaren ein, er läßt ihm in seinen Bildern auch immer soviel Raum, wie er braucht, um sich nicht gefangen, um sich frei und leicht zu fühlen.

Letztlich ist es das Spiel der Differenzen zwischen Zuständen und Dingen, dem wir den stimulierenden Reiz der Fotografien verdanken. Hamanns Bilder gewinnen in dem Maß an Bedeutung, in dem man ihnen die Freiheit zubilligt, die Verhältnisse von Bestimmtheit und Offenheit in der Schwebe zu lassen.

Gelingt eine Fotografie, dann teilen Fotograf und Betrachter das Glück, das sich daraus ergibt. Der Fotograf ist zufrieden, und der Betrachter ist dankbar, was letztlich auf das gleiche hinausläuft. Denn der Fotograf ist dankbar für das Talent und die unbekannte Kraft, die es ihm möglich gemacht hat, das Bild zu schaffen. Und der Betrachter ist dankbar für das Werk, das sein Verlangen befriedigt. Jeder visuelle Mensch hat diese Erfahrung gemacht und sich in seinem Leben an ein paar guten Bildern bereichert. Schlechte Bilder sollte man schnell wieder vergessen. Was allerdings gute Bilder ausmacht, ist schwer zu beschreiben. Es ist wie bei einem schönen Wein. Messen, wiegen oder zählen kann man das nicht, was einen herausragenden Tropfen charakterisiert. Es gibt am Schluß nur einen Weg, um hinter das Geheimnis der Qualität zu kommen, nämlich: trinken, trinken und nochmals trinken. So ähnlich ist es auch hier. Nur wer sich viel ansieht, nur wer das vergleichende Sehen übt, wird seine Freude und Erkenntnis steigern können. Natürlich muß man über gute Bilder und seine Erfahrungen mit diesen reden, muß sich gegenseitig sagen, was man sieht, denkt und empfindet. Und zwar genau in dieser Reihenfolge. Nur zu sehen, nur zu denken, nur zu empfinden, führt nicht weit. Vladimir Nabokov hat immer wieder empfohlen, ein gutes Buch nicht nur mit dem Herzen zu lesen. Das Herz wäre ein bemerkenswert dummer Leser, meinte Nabokov. Aber auch mit dem Gehirn allein solle man sich nicht einem Werk der Kunst nähern, sondern mit dem Gehirn und der Wirbelsäule. In Wahrheit sagt uns das Prickeln entlang der Wirbelsäule, was der Fotograf bei einem gelungenen Bild empfunden hat und uns empfinden zu lassen wünscht. Fast unnötig zu erwähnen, daß die Wirbelsäule vertikal verläuft.

Andreas Bee
(Museum für Moderne Kunst, Frankfurt/Main)

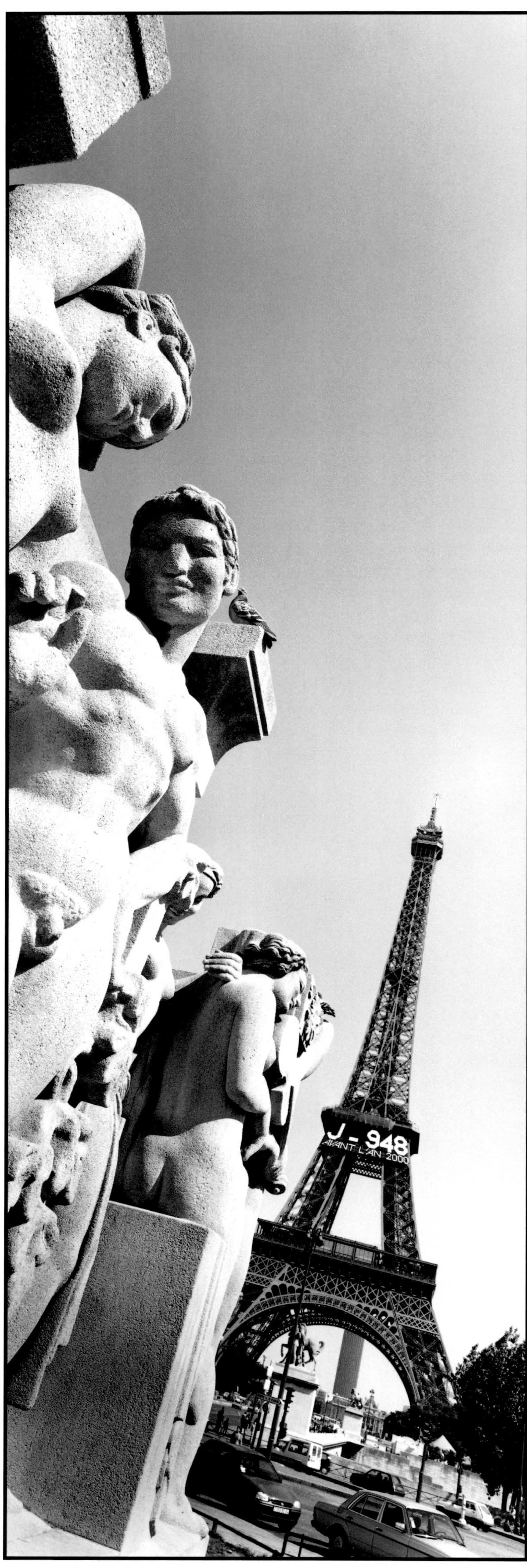

Trocadero, Tour Eiffel, Paris 1997

Les images, dit-on, sont des fenêtres ouvertes sur un monde particulier qui souvent paraît étrange. Des bonnes images on dit également qu'elles ne dégagent pas seulement la perspective d'une autre réalité, mais même qu'elles ouvrent l'accès aux profonds alignements de l'espace et aux larges panoramas des paysages. Si l'une de ces images réussies nous attire au point de faire naître l'envie d'y rentrer et d'oublier pour un instant notre monde réel, nous devons nous efforcer de trouver une voie par laquelle nous pouvons pénétrer dans ce monde particulier de l'image. Imaginons donc que, tel un cambrioleur ou un amoureux en cachette, nous pénétrons, avec concentration et précaution, à travers l'une de ces fenêtres séductrices, dans l'espace présenté par l'image. Dès l'instant où nous enjambons en souplesse le rebord de la fenêtre et franchissons le seuil entre l'ici et le là, le cadre du tableau disparaît de notre vue. Nous sommes dans l'image. Dès lors que nous avons changé de coté, nous pouvons, pour un temps, oublier d'où nous sommes venus et nous pouvons nous adonner entièrement au monde artificiel qui devient pour nous le monde réel. Seulement, en général nous ne pouvons y séjourner longtemps. Aussi réussie que soit cette perception, elle sera trop instable. Tôt ou tard la réalité nous rappelle. Nous refranchissons la fenêtre par laquelle nous sommes venus un instant plus tôt. Et le cadre disparaît une deuxième fois au moment du passage vers l'ancienne réalité.

Par analogie avec les prises de vue traditionnelles qui fonctionnent comme des fenêtres, les "Vertical Views" de Horst Hamann peuvent se comparer à des portes hautes et étroites. Certaines semblent s'ouvrir vers l'extérieur, d'autres vers l'intérieur. Il y en a qui ne sont qu'entrebaillées. De celles-là le spectateur s'approche avec hésitation. La plupart cependant semblent être une véritable invitation, comme des écluses largement ouvertes et passantes et elles attirent le spectateur presque imperceptiblement dans l'espace imagé. Non seulement son regard évidemment, mais le spectateur en entier, en tant que sujet vertical. Face aux oeuvres de Horst Hamann personne n'a besoin d'escalader pour trouver l'entrée par une fenêtre visuelle ou intellectuelle. L'impressionnant de ces images à format haut c'est leur ouverture et accessibilité. Cette particularité résulte du pivotement de la caméra panoramique classique de la position horizontale à la verticale, un procédé qui paraît si simpliste et formaliste. C'est cette volte-face si simple mais indicatrice de nouvelles perspectives qui a un effet tout à fait surprenant et fait de la fenêtre une porte.

Que peut-on des expériences faites dans l'image faire valoir dans la vie de tous les jours? Difficile à dire. Peu sans doute au rapport 1:1. Mais la plupart des spectateurs qui se sont laissés entrainer ne serait-ce qu'une fois entièrement par les images verticales de Horst Hamann ont une autre façon de vivre une promenade à travers la ville de New York, de Hongkong ou de Paris, avec d'autres regards, sentiments et attentes. Il est même

Le picotement le long de la colonne vertébrale

possible que dorénavant le format d'une photographie ne leur sera plus jamais indifférent. Puisqu'ils ont fait l'expérience qu'il peut être très facile d'entrer dans l'image sans avoir absolument besoin d'une échelle ou d'autres moyens de secours.

L'expérience décisive qui a amené Hamann au changement de paradigme eut lieu en 1991 au Bryant Park à la 41ème rue de New York. Avec une caméra panoramique Linhof il prenait d'abord des vues horizontales assez conventionnelles, pas très satisfaisantes, avec en arrière-plan le skyline de la métropole. Toutes ces prises paraissaient comme des vues limitées à travers les meurtrières d'un char blindé. Lorsque Hamann, par curiosité et l'envie d'expérimenter, fit pivoter la caméra de 90°, il reçut subitement des images qui se distinguaient de façon choquante du résultat des prises horizontales du même environnement. Tout à coup le paysage urbain, jusque là une barre lourde, s'ouvrit à la vue. Alors que le format oblong faisait paraître le skyline très loin et l'accès à l'espace présenté difficile, le format vertical réduit à un minimum la distance entre l'image et le spectateur.

Pour décisif que fût le changement de la perspective en passant de l'horizontale à la verticale, il n'explique pas à lui seul l'attraction des images de Horst Hamann. La distribution de la lumière, le modelage prononcé du clair-obscur et les tons de gris soigneusement calculés jouent évidemment aussi un rôle décisif. Dans ces prises verticales en noir et blanc, Hamann s'appuie également sur les valeurs qui semblent presque classiques, comme la structure, la composition, l'équilibre des proportions, l'intensité et le raffinement. Indépendamment du format que l'on ne peut évidemment jamais séparer du contenu pour ces prises, ces images peuvent se comparer à des portes ouvertes et même, à titre expérimental, à des surfaces savamment tendues. Des surfaces sur lesquelles la forme objective et visible s'entrechoque avec la contemplation subjective personnelle et où cette collision crée, par les oeuvres les plus réussies, des vibrations à résonance durable. Pour le dire plus concrètement, la vue de la gorge profonde d'une rue de New York présentée sous verre et dans un cadre représente cette surface tendue évoquée. En la comparant à une peau de tambour fortement tendue qui reste muette jusqu'au moment où l'engagement d'un spectateur la mettra en vibration.

Ce qui frappe, c'est le nombre de photographies de Hamann qui ouvrent une vue au loin malgré les compositions qui remplissent le cadre. On pourrait croire par moments que cette ouverture vers l'espace est un accord de base discret mais présent dans toutes ses oeuvres. Même le joueur de basket remplissant entièrement le cadre évoque devant l'oeil intérieur un mouvement libre dans une large espace. Non seulement Horst Hamann fait entrer le spectateur avec tout son corps, mais encore il lui laisse à l'intérieur de l'image l'espace dont il a besoin pour ne pas se sentir prisonnier mais libre et léger.

En fin de compte c'est au jeu des différences entre états et objets que nous devons le charme stimulant de ses oeuvres. Les photographies de Hamann prennent de l'importance pour nous à mesure que nous leur accordons la liberté de laisser en suspens les rapports entre la certitude et l'ouverture. Si une photographie est réussie, le bonheur qui en résulte se partage entre le photographe et le spectateur. Le photographe est content et le spectateur est reconnaissant, ce qui, en définitive, revient au même. Car le photographe est reconnaissant pour son talent et pour la force inconnue qui l'ont rendu capable de créer l'oeuvre. Et le spectateur est reconnaissant pour l'oeuvre qui assouvit son désir. Toute personne visuelle a déjà fait cette expérience et s'est enrichie dans sa vie par quelques belles images. Quant aux mauvaises, on devrait les oublier vite. Mais il est difficile de définir ce qui fait d'une image une bonne image. C'est comme pour un bon vin. Impossible de mesurer, peser ou compter ce qui caractérise un bon cru. Il n y a finalement qu'un chemin pour percer le secret de sa qualité: boire, boire et boire encore. Même pour l'art c'est ainsi. Seul celui qui regarde beaucoup et qui s'entraine au regard comparatif pourra accroître sa joie et sa connaissance. Bien sûr, il faut parler des bonnes images et des expériences que l'on fait avec elles; il faut se dire ce que l'on voit, pense et sent. Et justement dans cet ordre. Voir seulement, penser ou sentir seulement, ne nous mène pas loin. Vladimir Nabokov a toujours recommandé de ne pas lire un bon livre uniquement avec le coeur. Selon lui le coeur est un lecteur stupide. Mais il ne faut pas non plus aborder une oeuvre d'art avec le seul cerveau; il faut le cerveau et la colonne vertébrale. En vérité, le picotement le long de la colonne vertébrale nous transmet ce que le photographe a senti en créant une image réussie et qu'il souhaite nous faire sentir. Il est sans doute inutile de rappeler que la colonne vertébrale est verticale.

Andreas Bee
(Museum für Moderne Kunst, Frankfurt/Main)

Golden Gate Bridge, Detail, San Francisco 2000

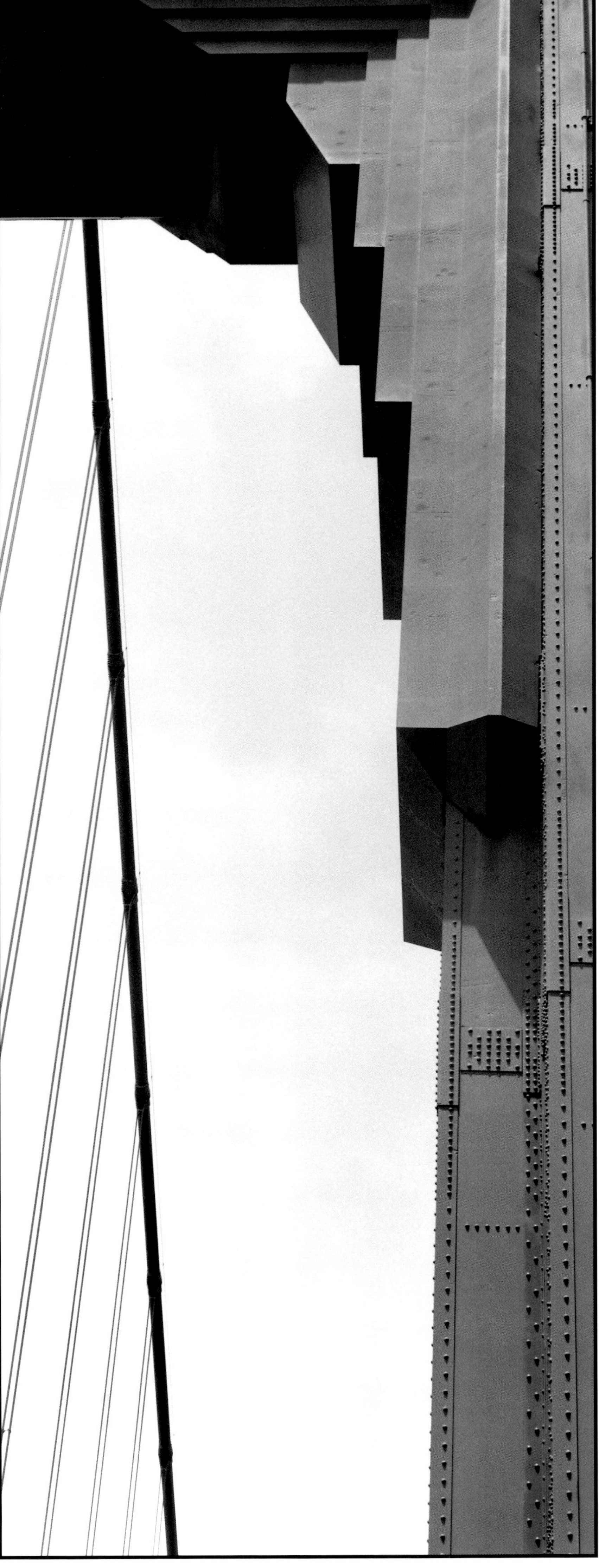

Pemaquid Light, Maine 2001

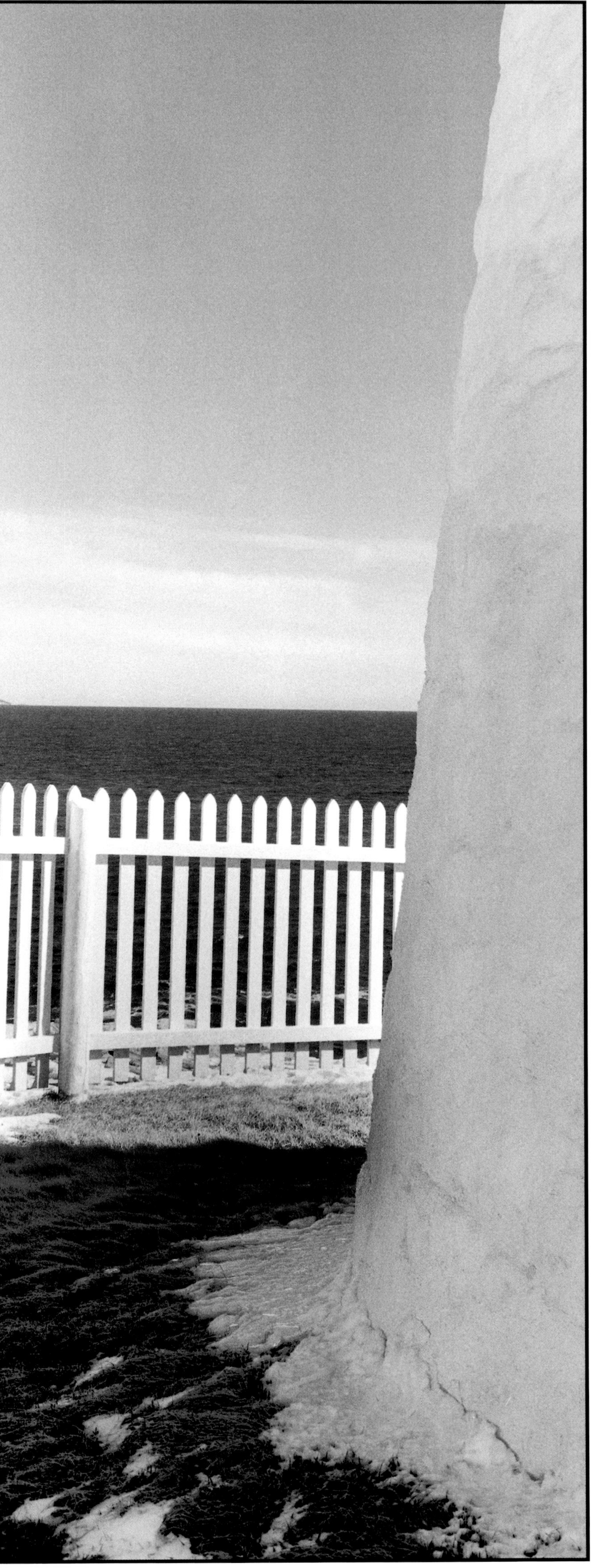

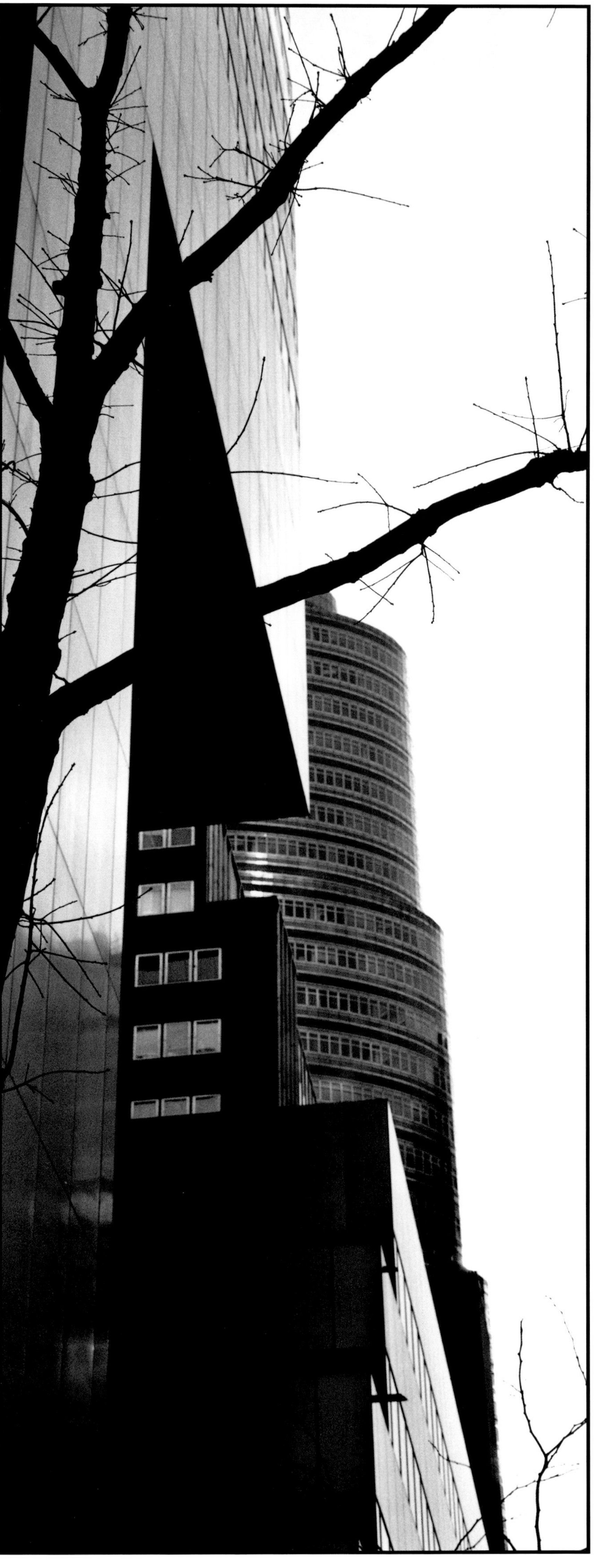

Royal Festival Hall, London 1999

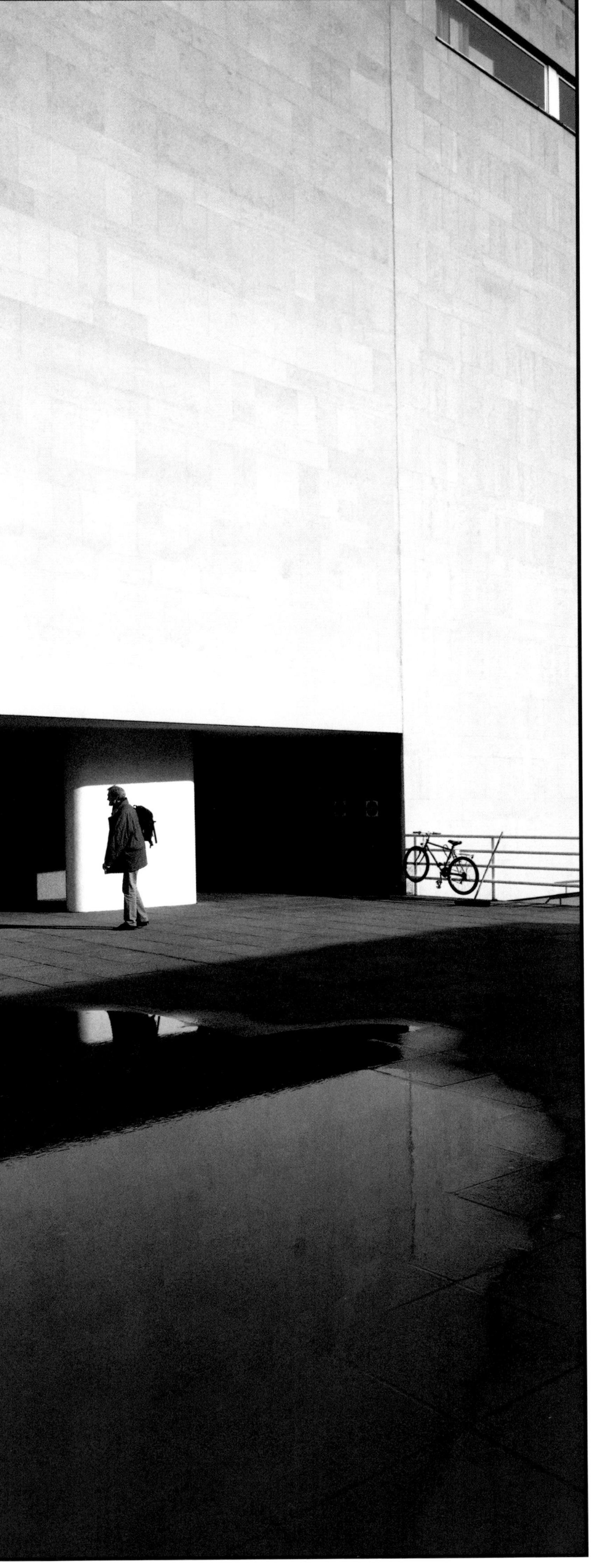

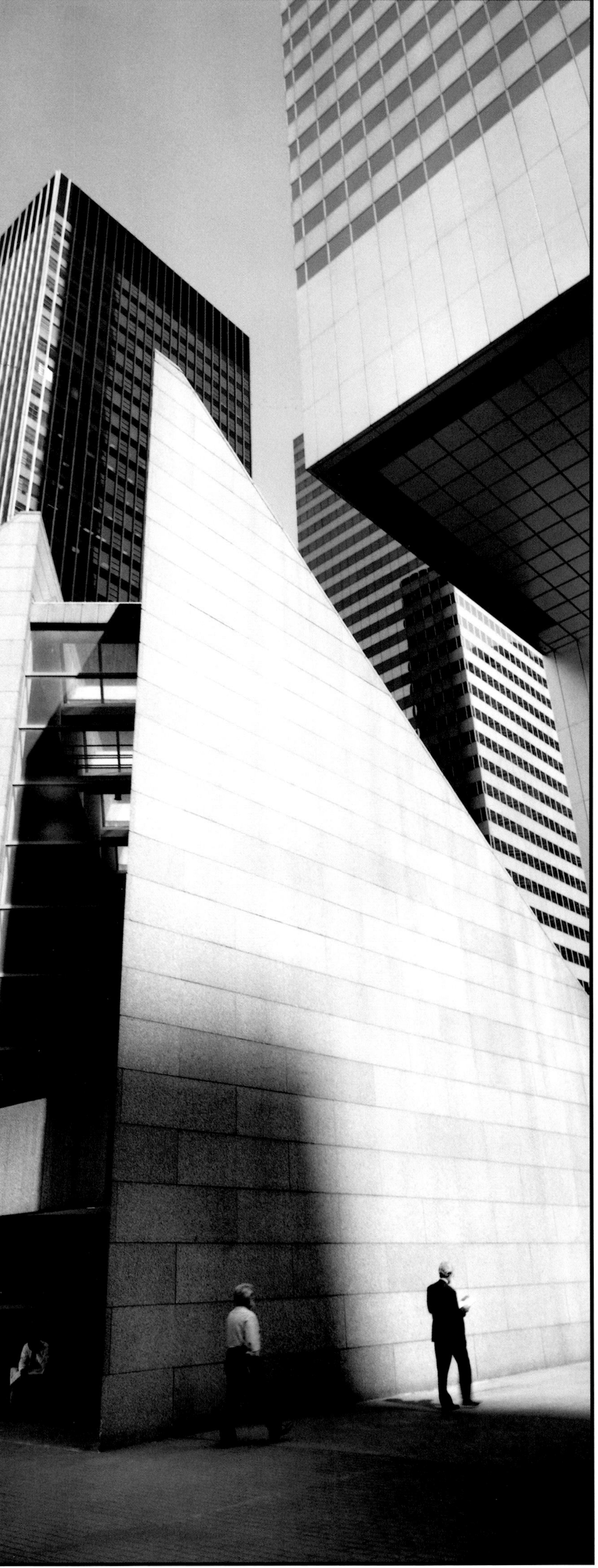

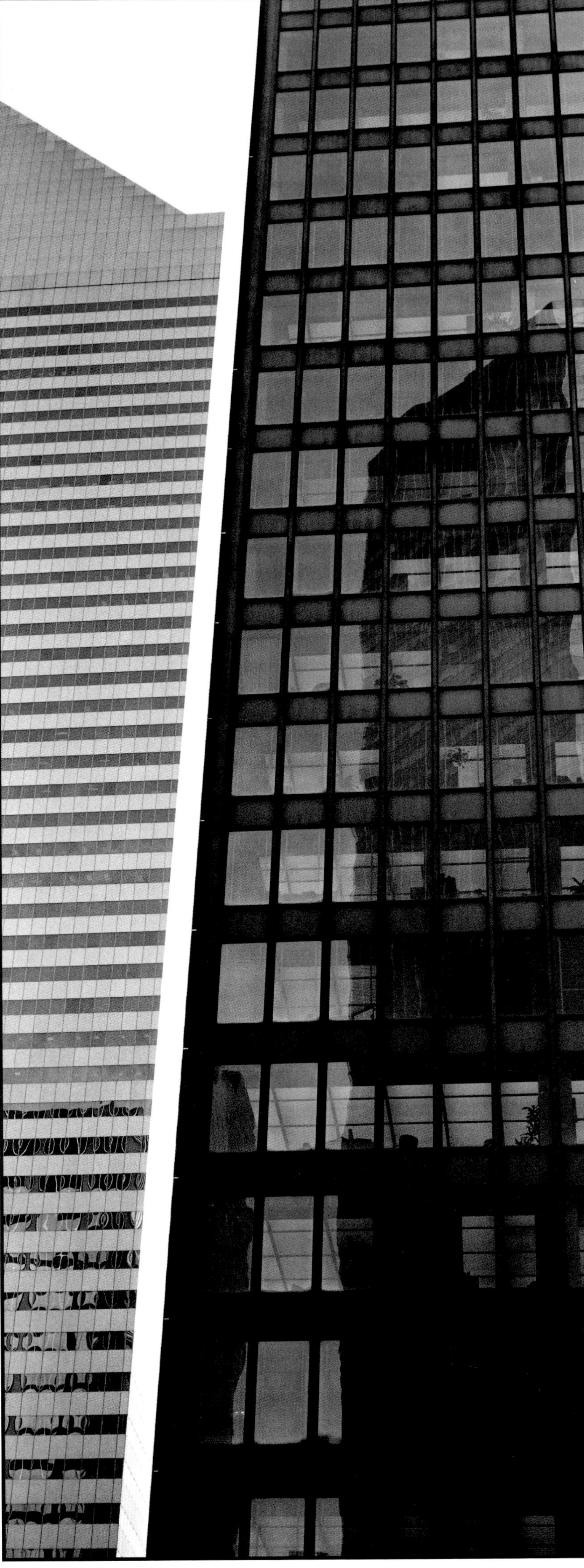

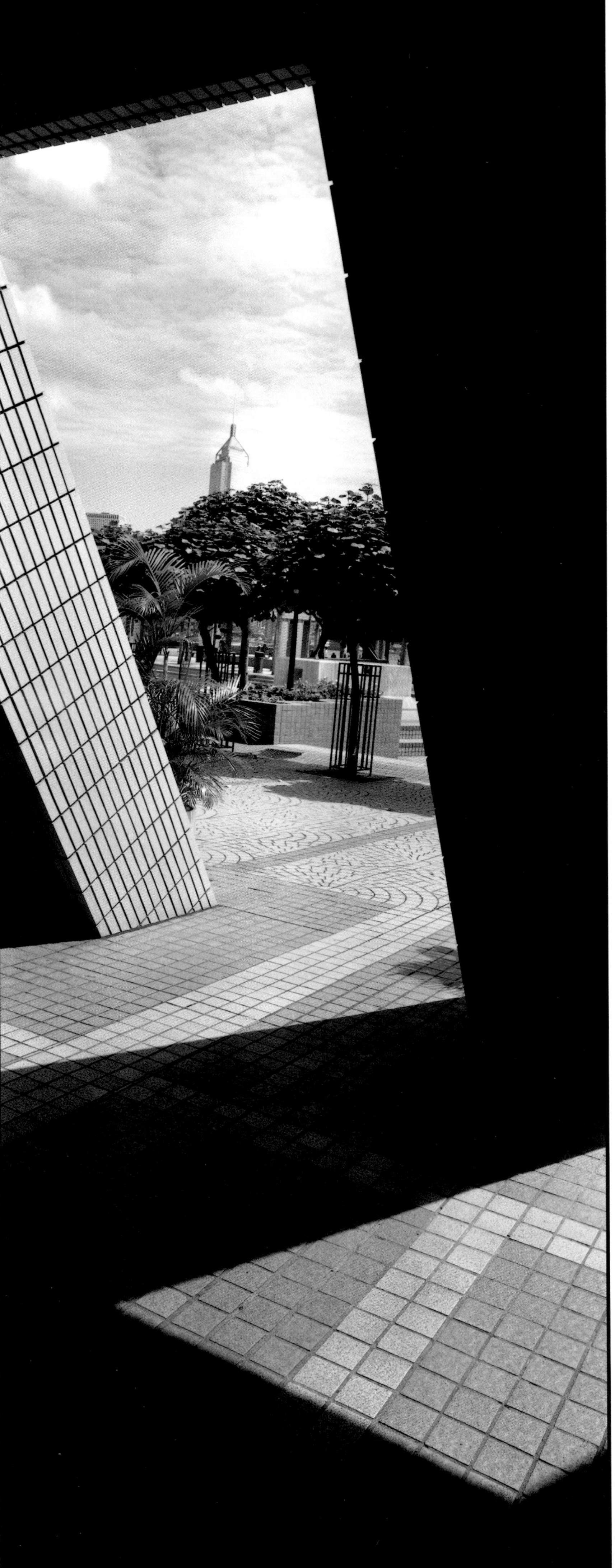

Clocktower, New York 1995

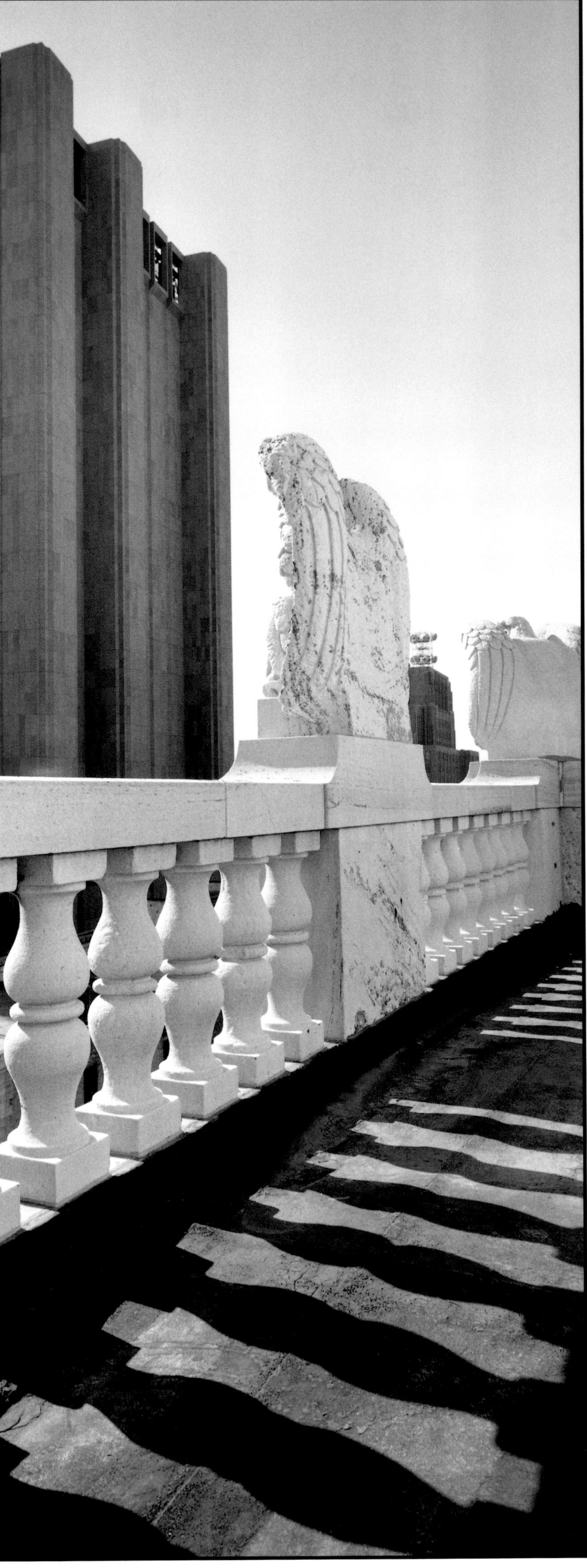

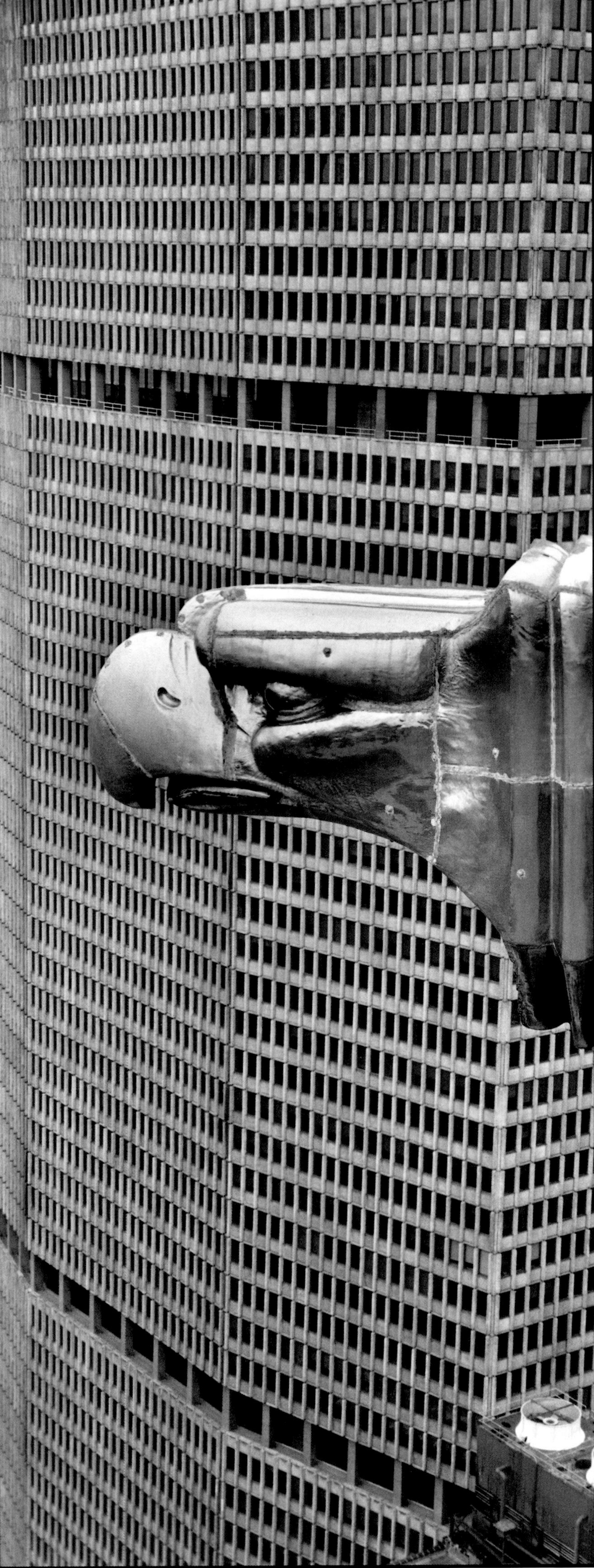

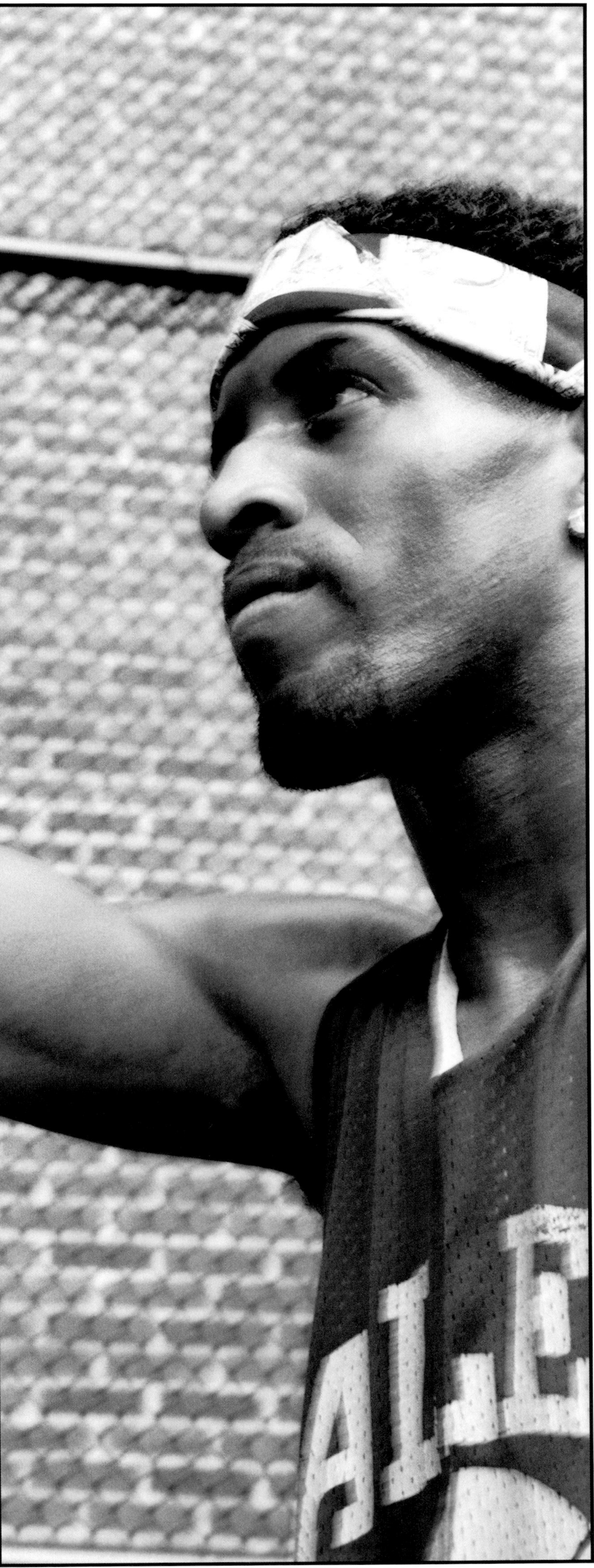

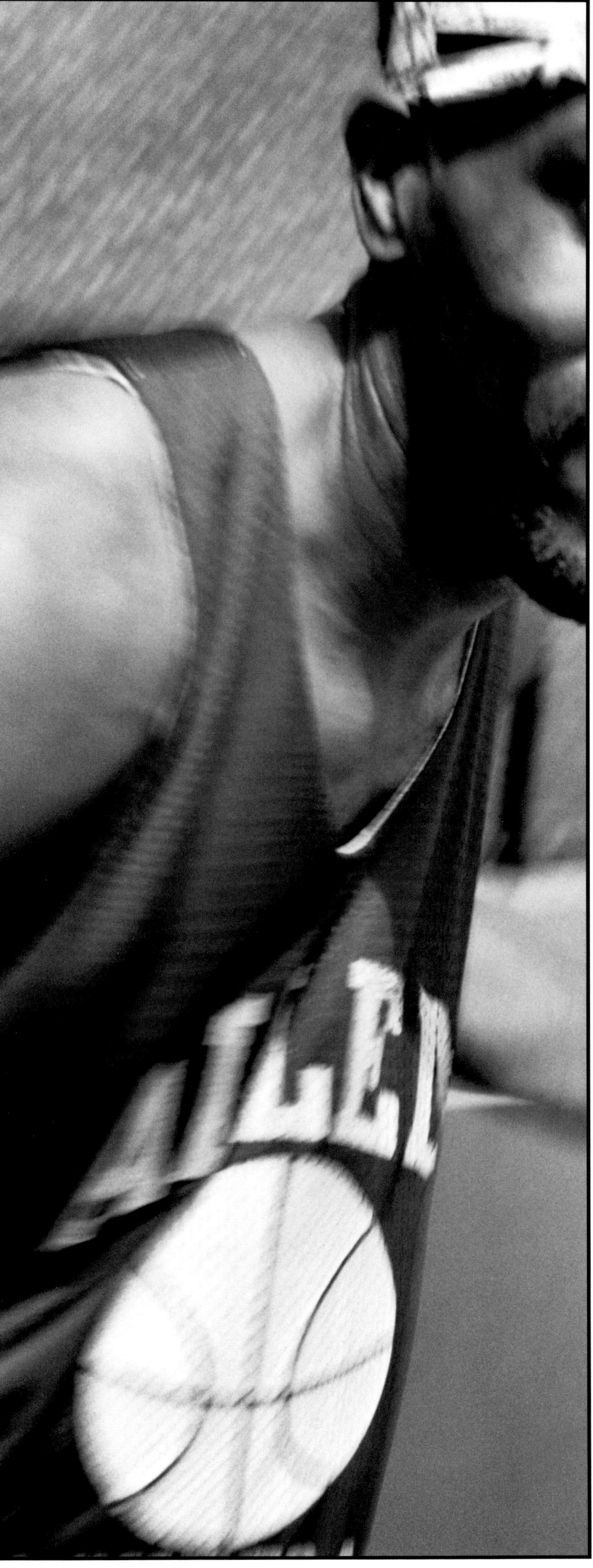

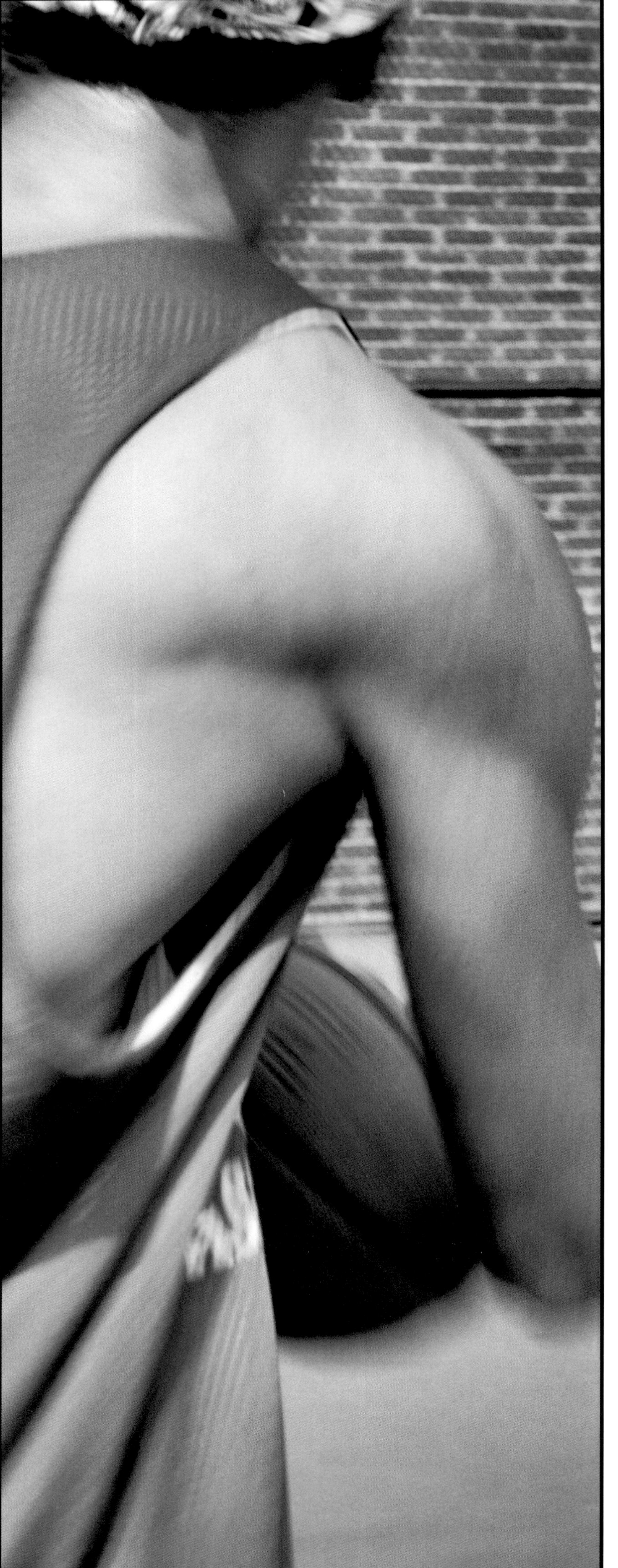

Jaimee, Back, New York 2000

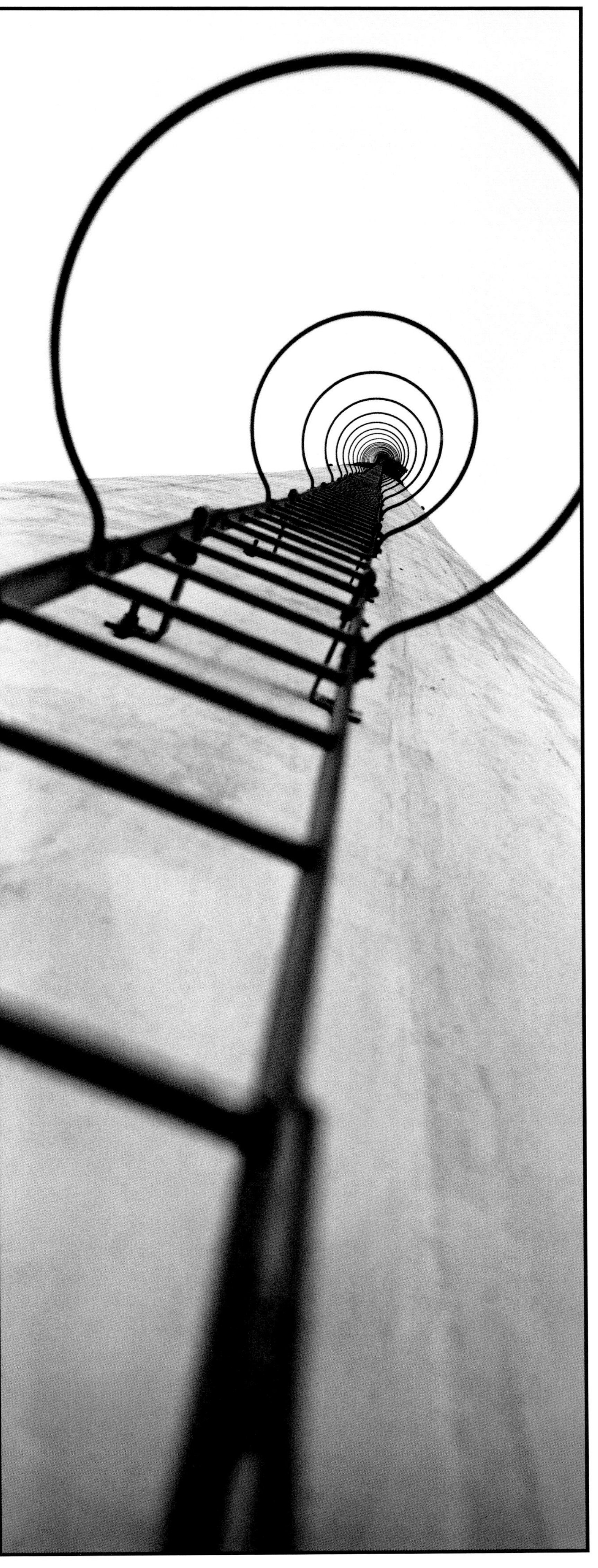

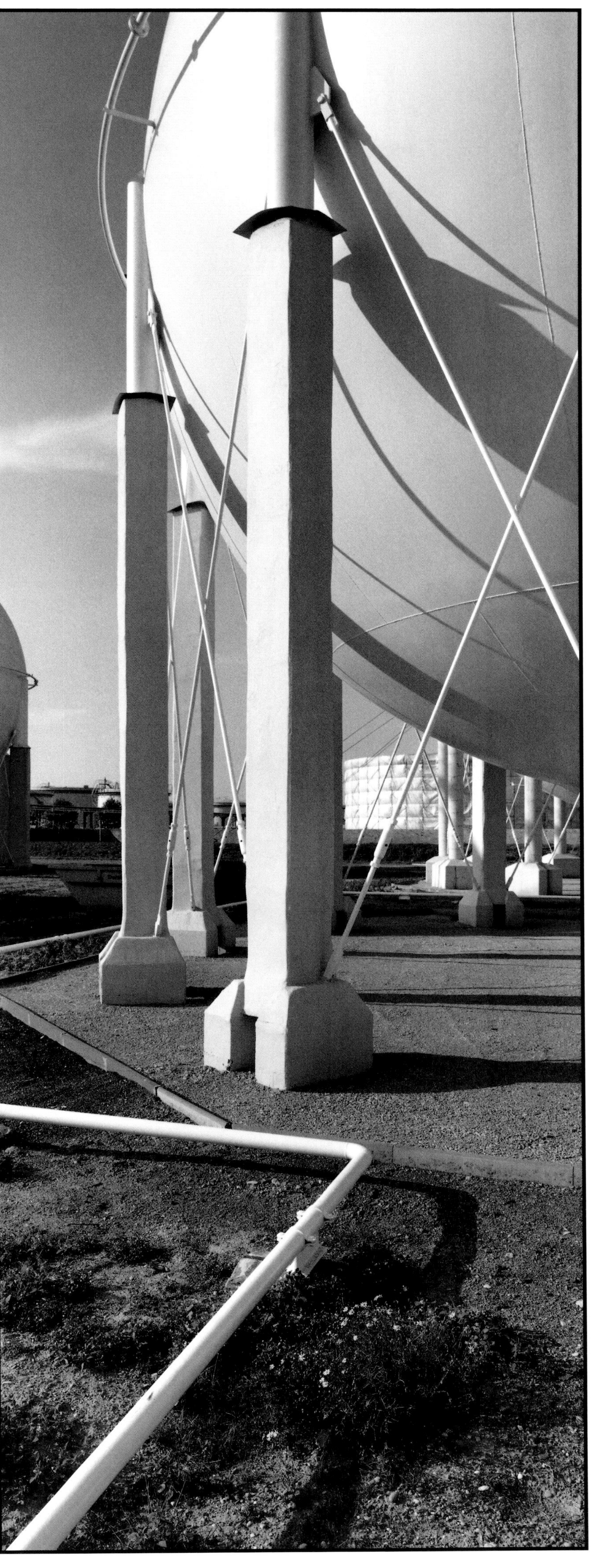

50

Museum of Modern Art, Interior, San Francisco 2000

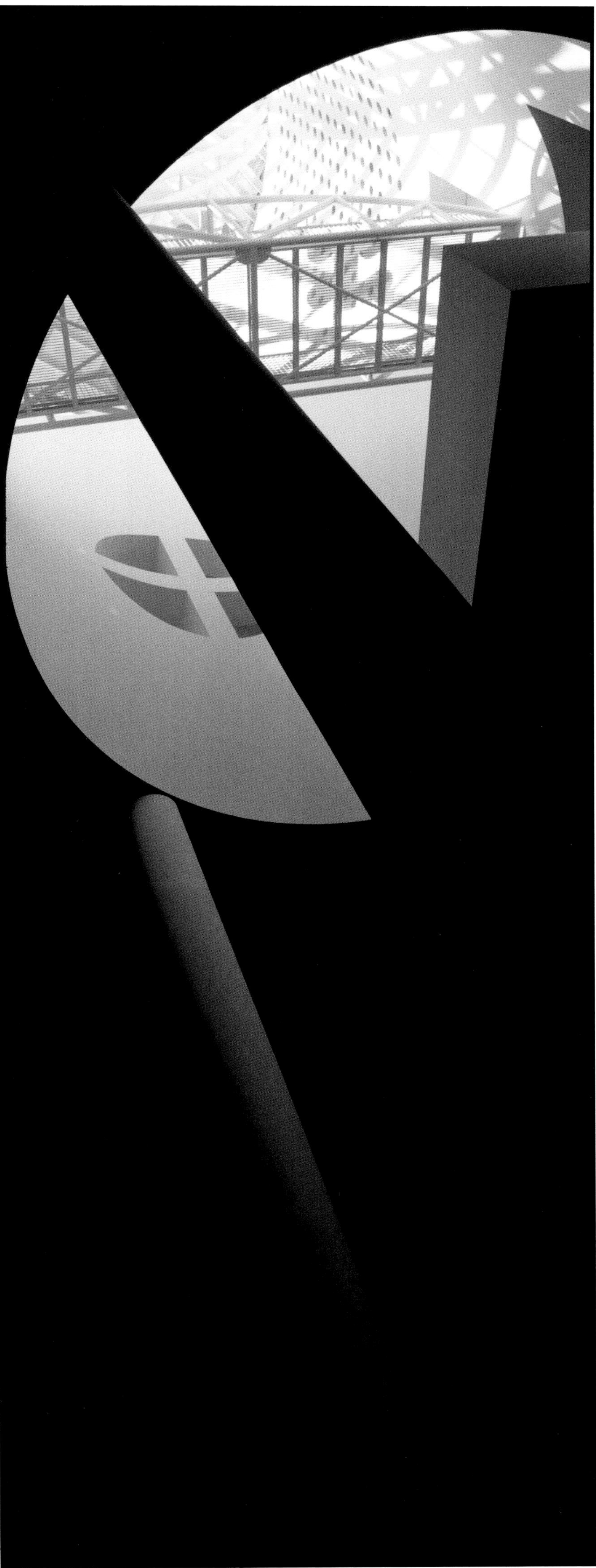

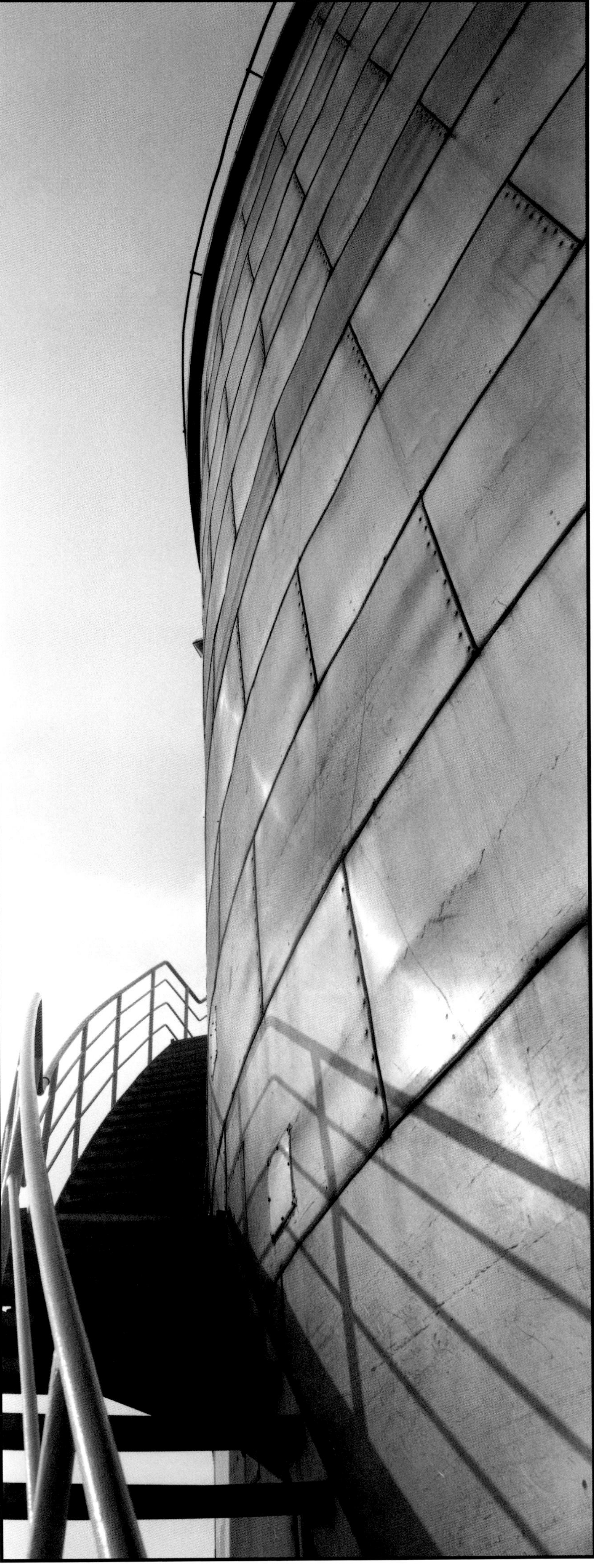

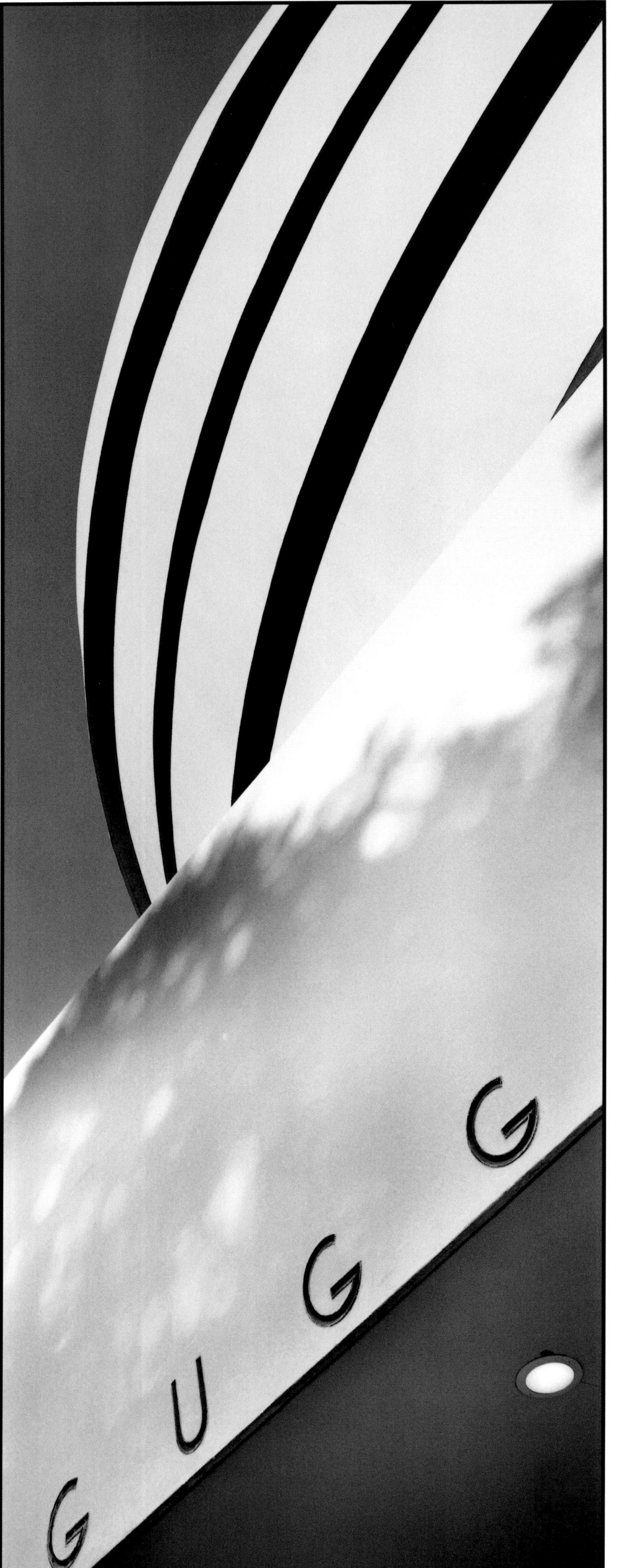

G
U
G
G
G

Solomon R. Guggenheim Museum, New York 1996

Solomon R. Guggenheim Museum, Interior, New York 2001

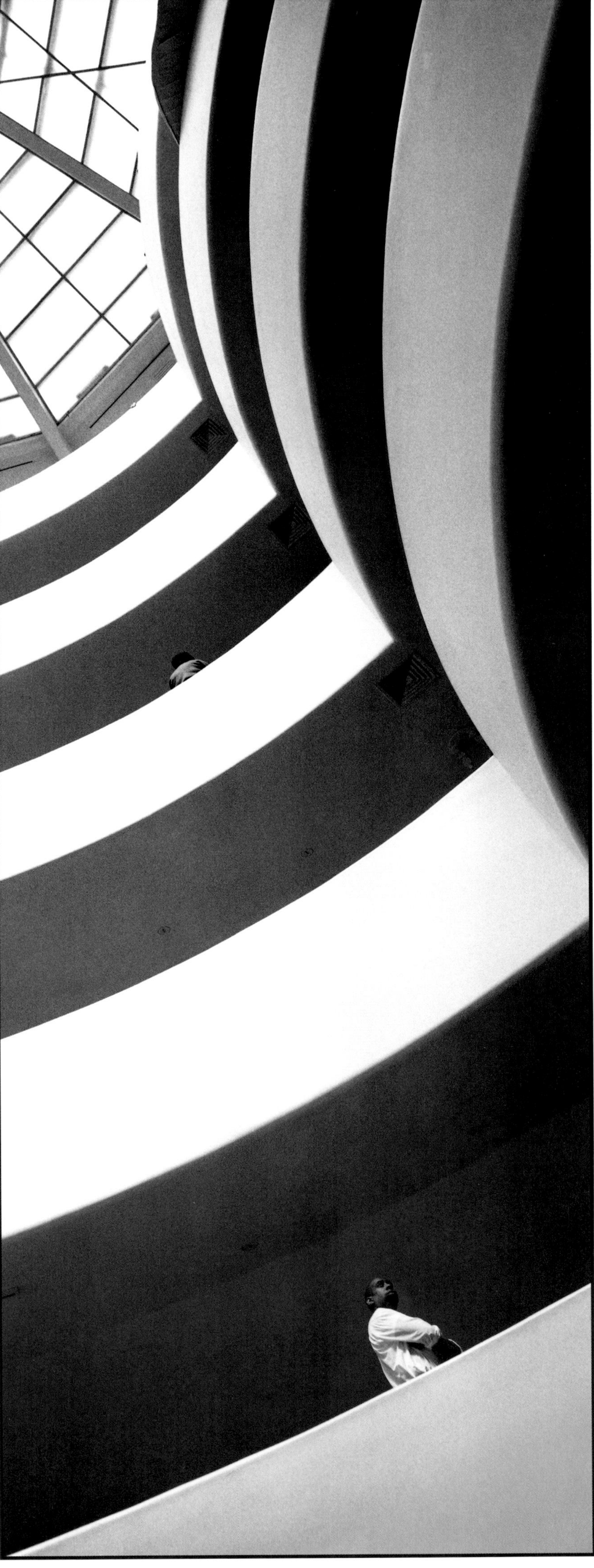

Twin Towers, New York 1996

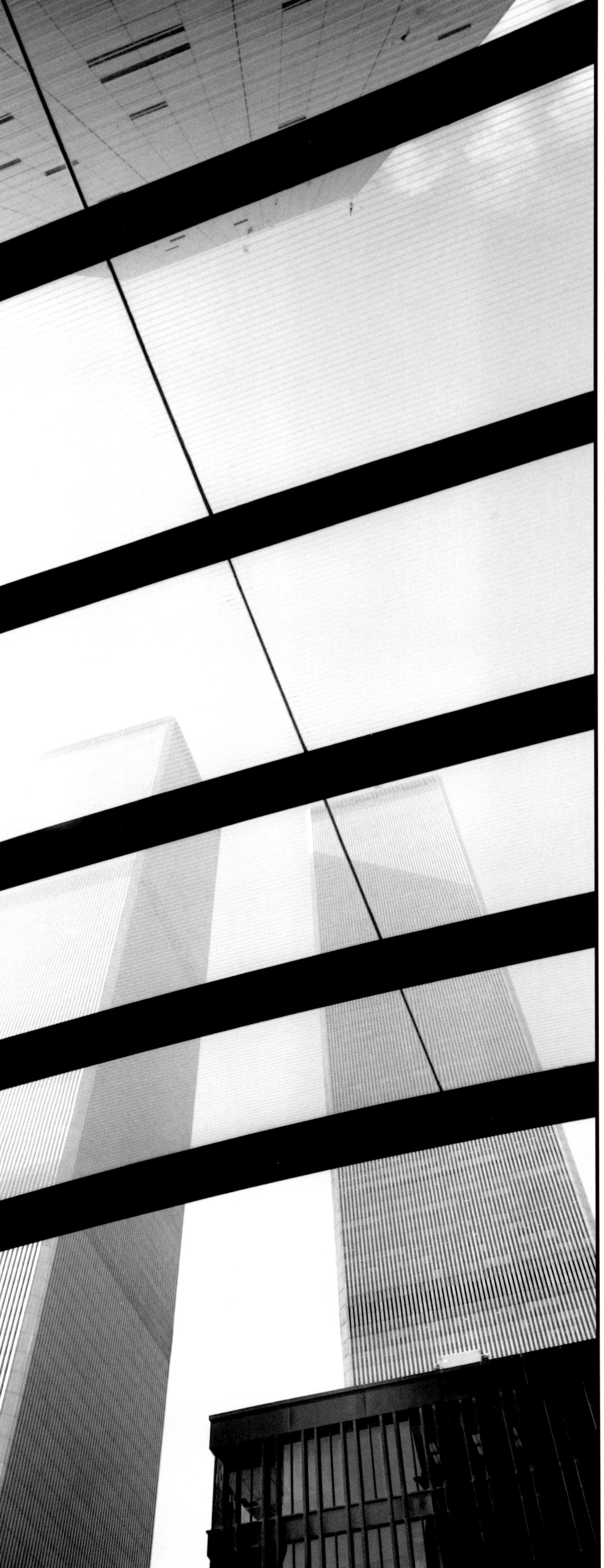

60

Tour Eiffel, Detail II, Paris 1999

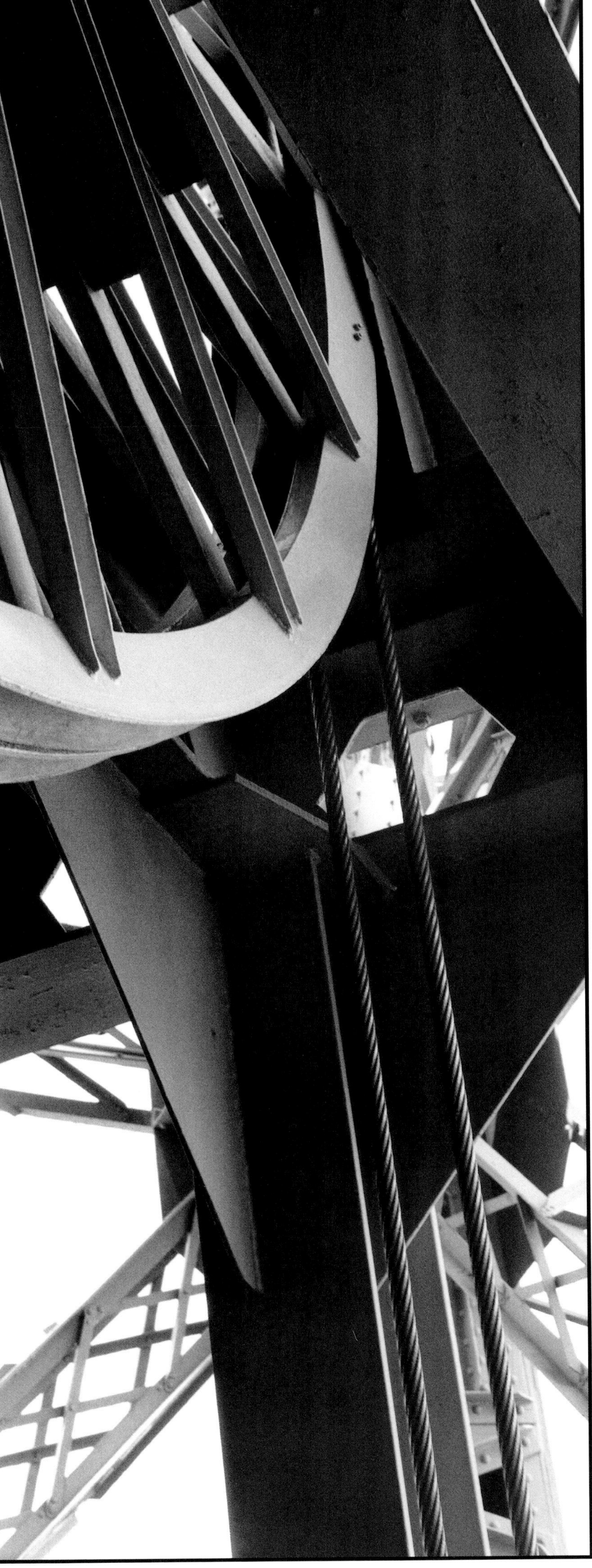

New England Aquarium, Boston 2001

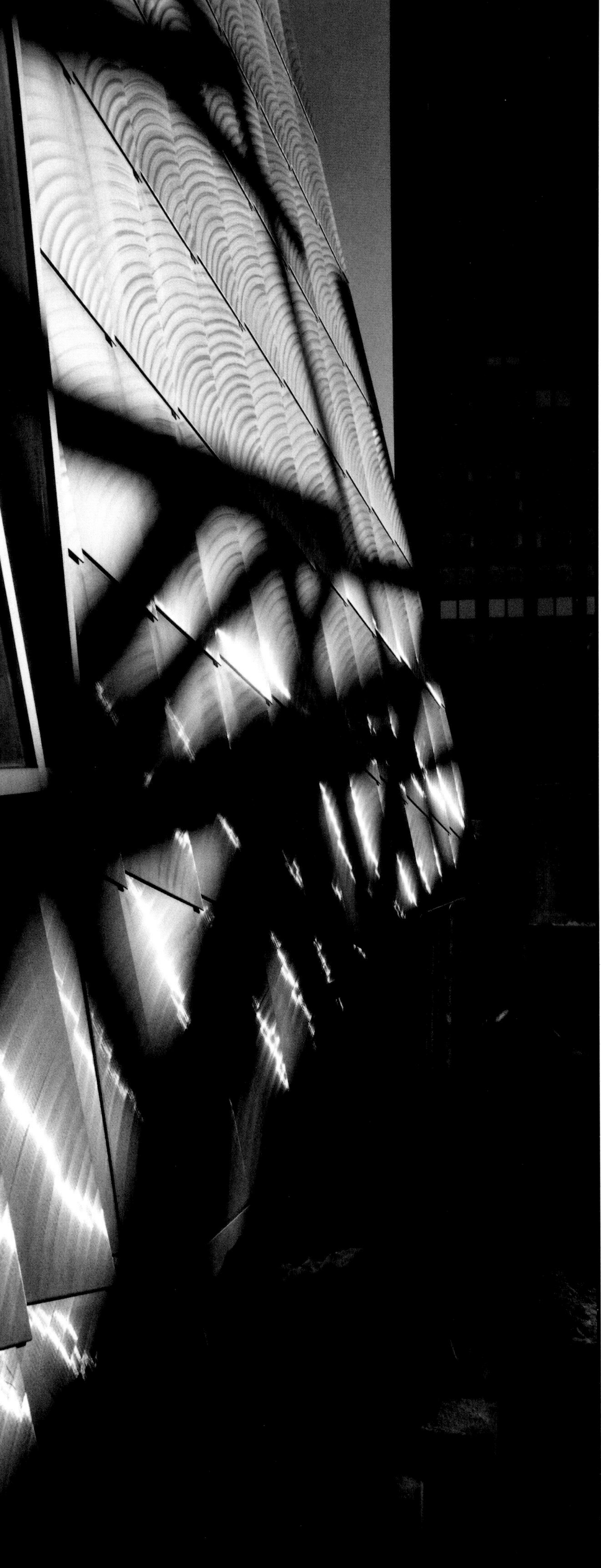

Victoria Peak, Hong Kong 1996

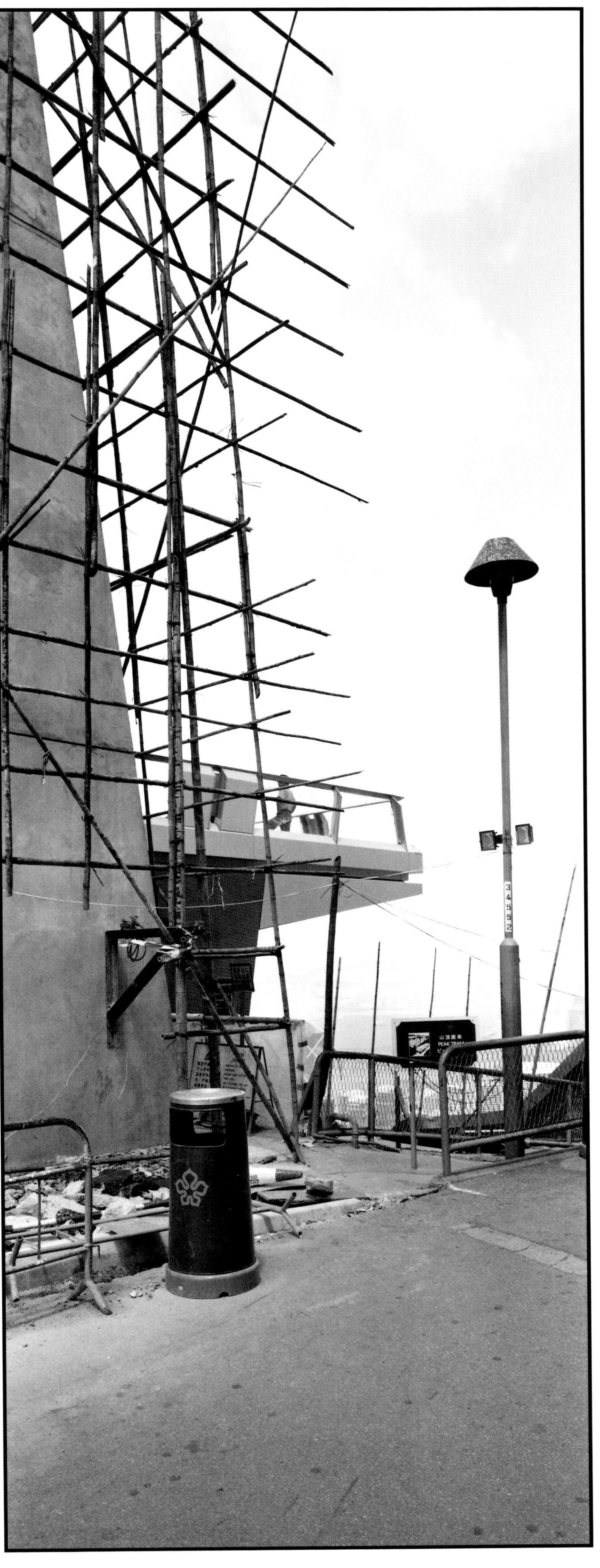

山頂纜車
PEAK TRAM
ピー
3455
2

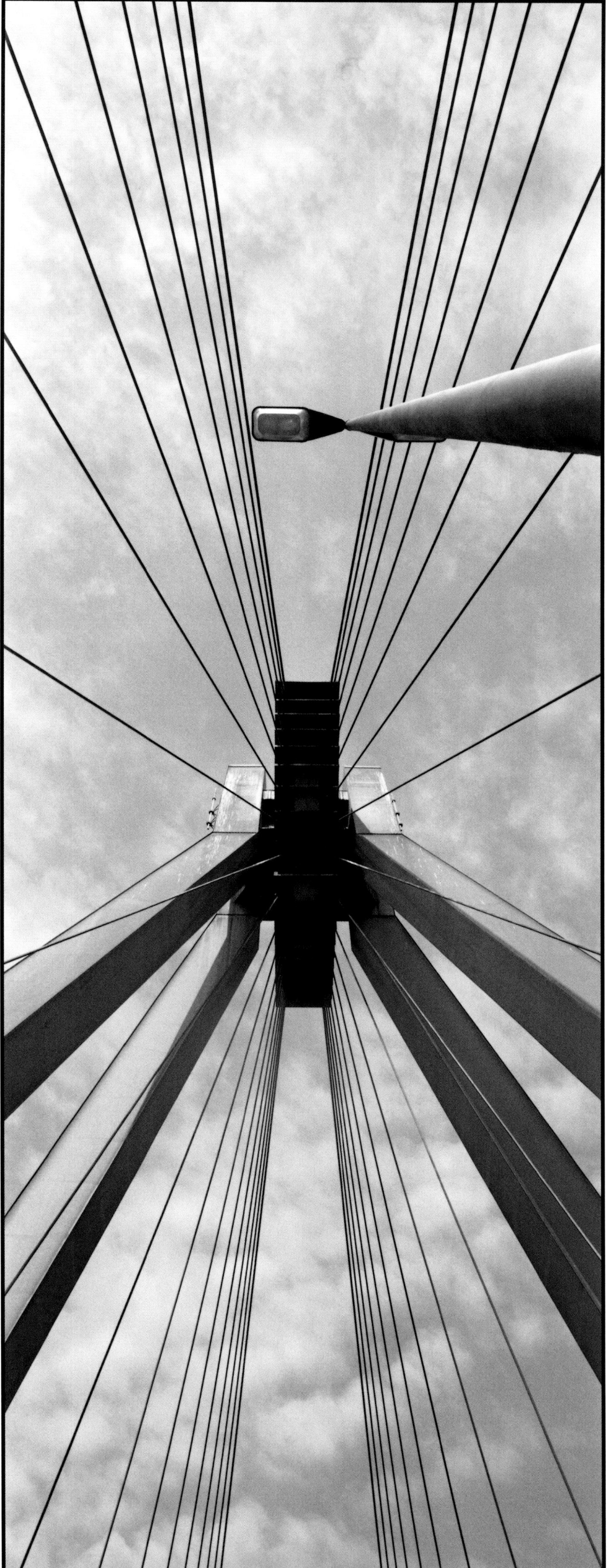

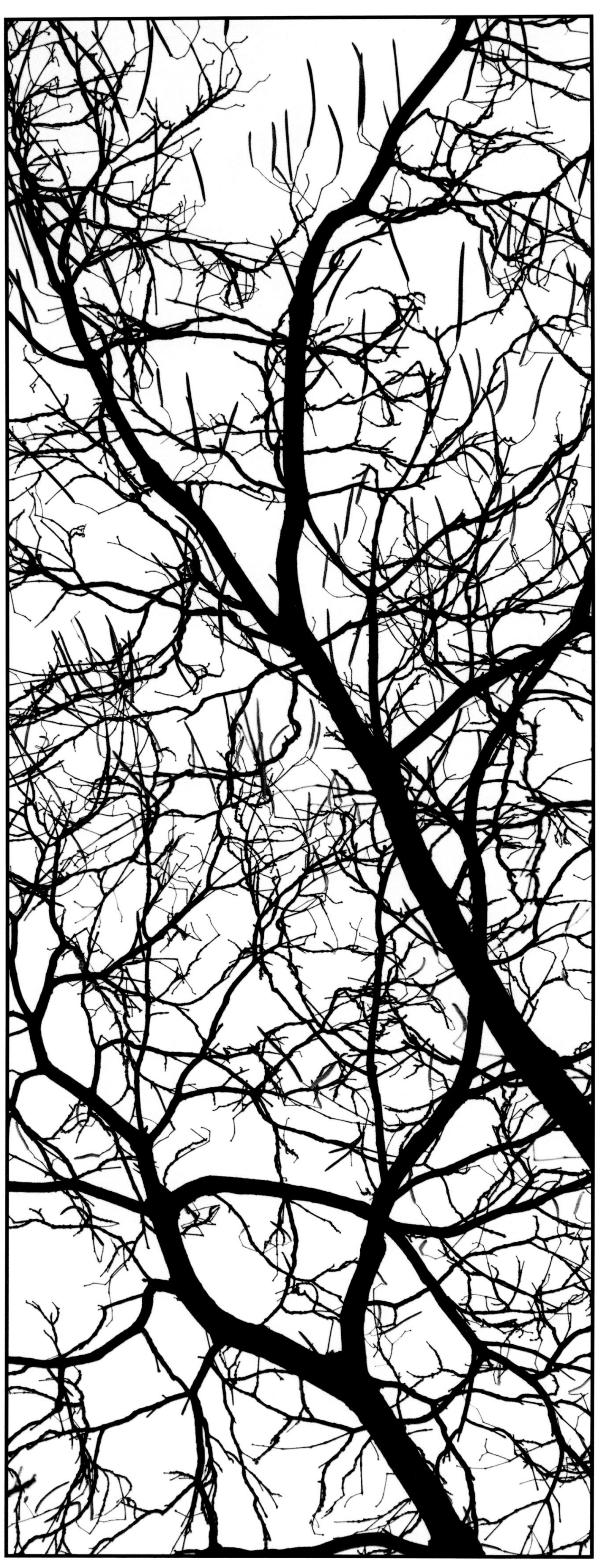

Tree Study, Ludwigshafen / Rh. 1999

Tour Eiffel, Northeast Pillar, Paris 1997

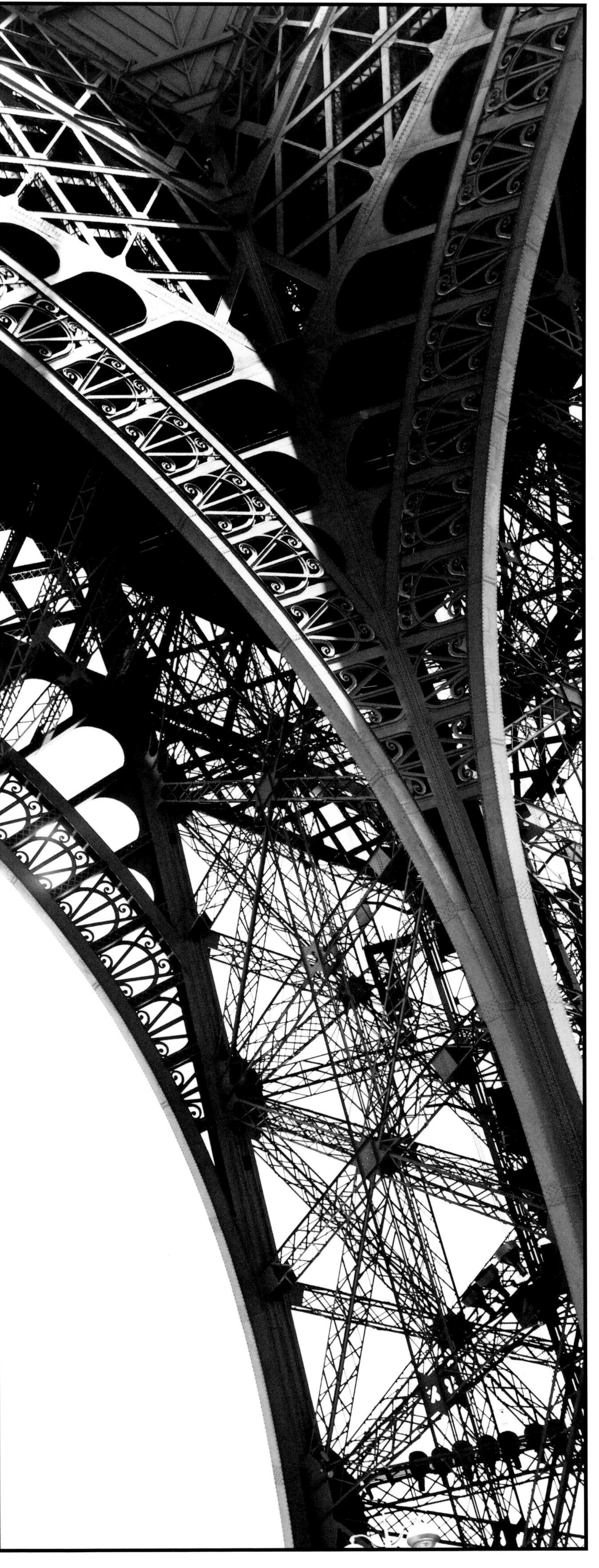

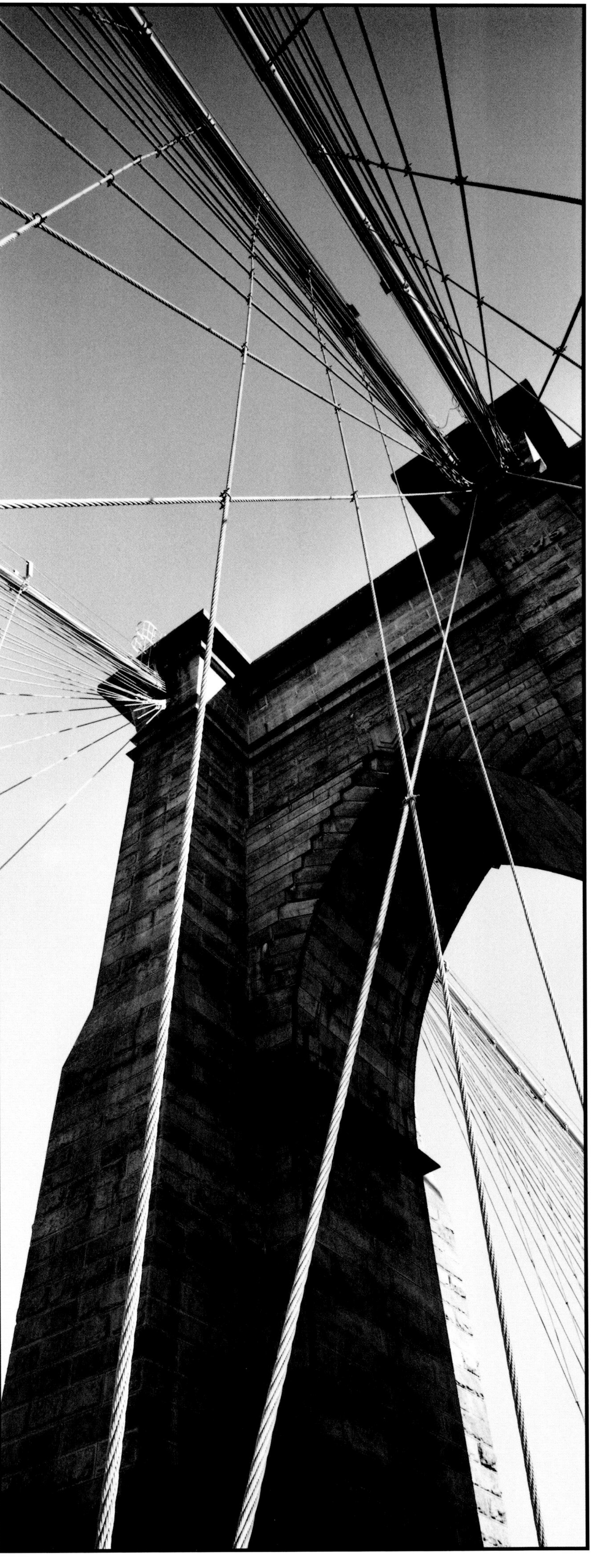

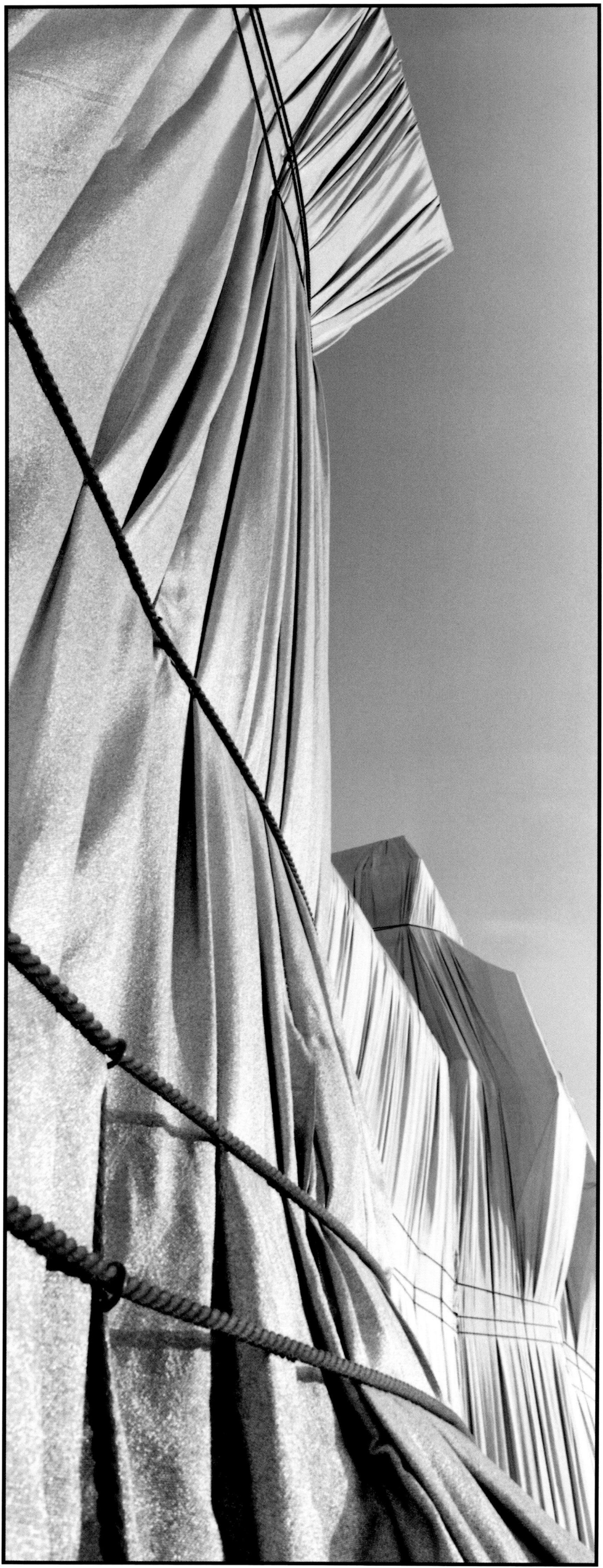

Christo, Wrapped Reichstag, Berlin 1995

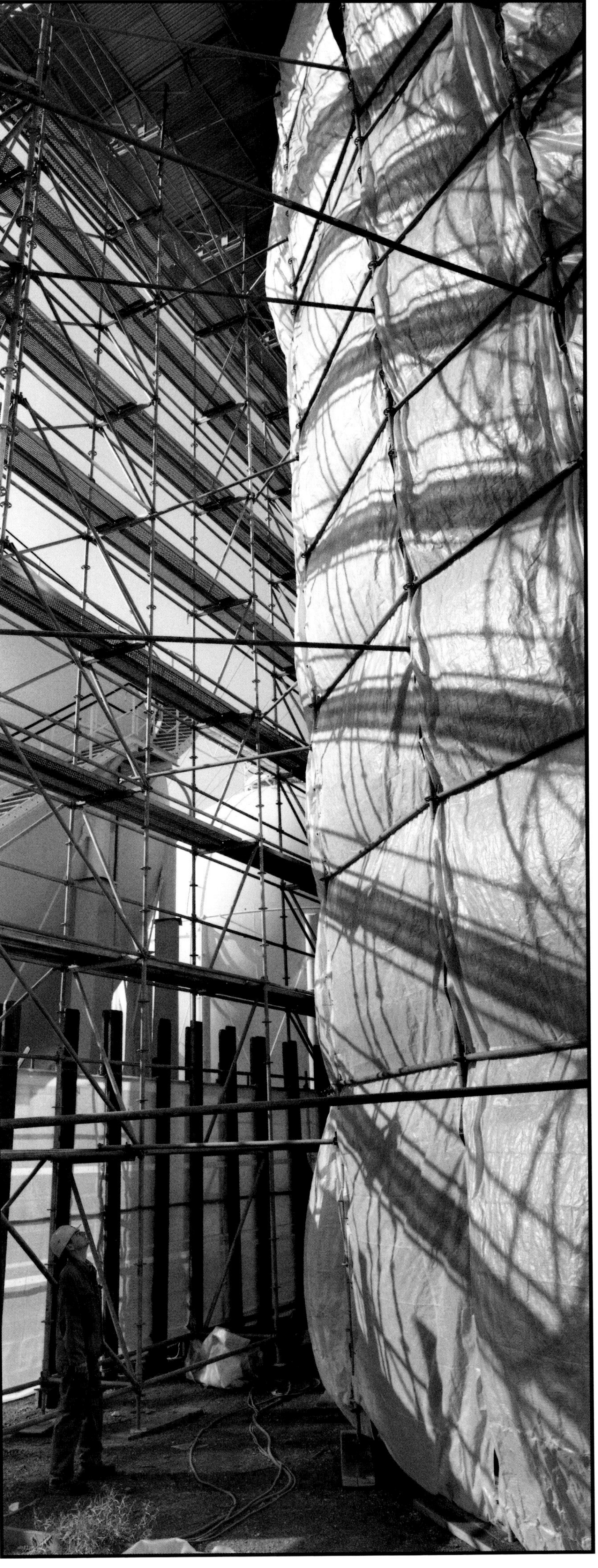

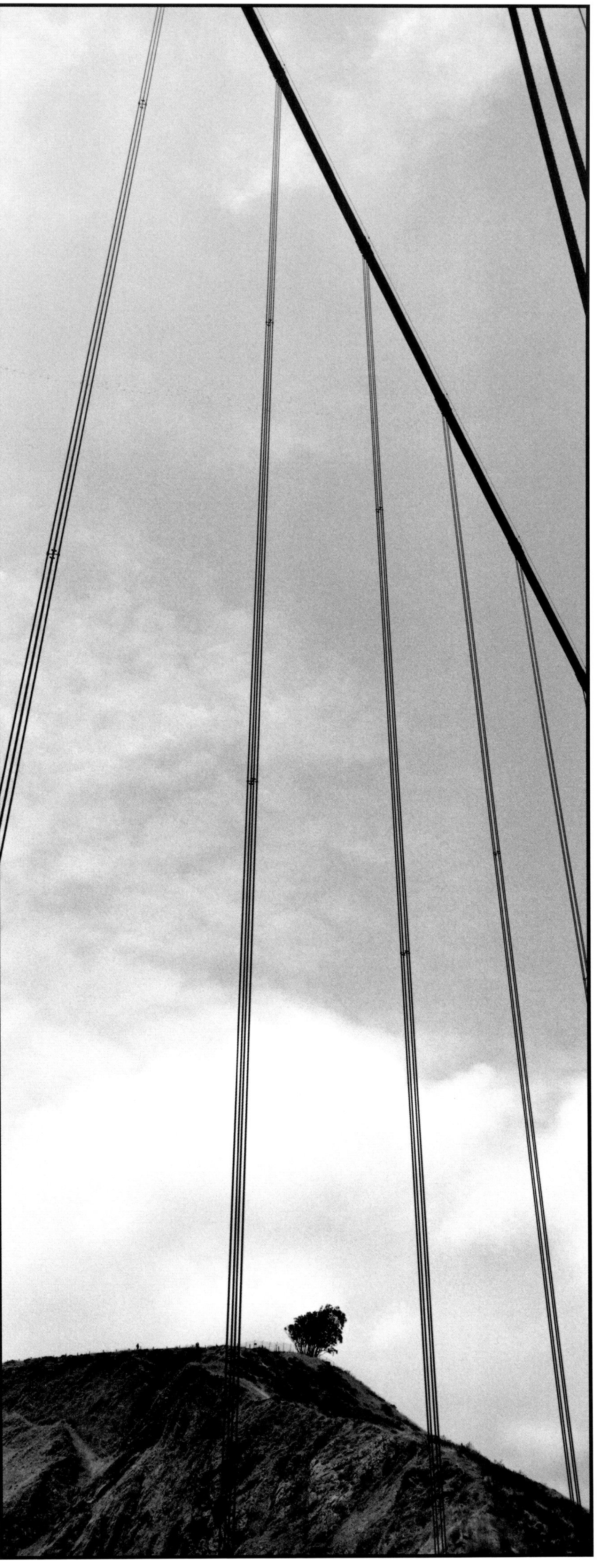

Les Tuileries, Paris 1998

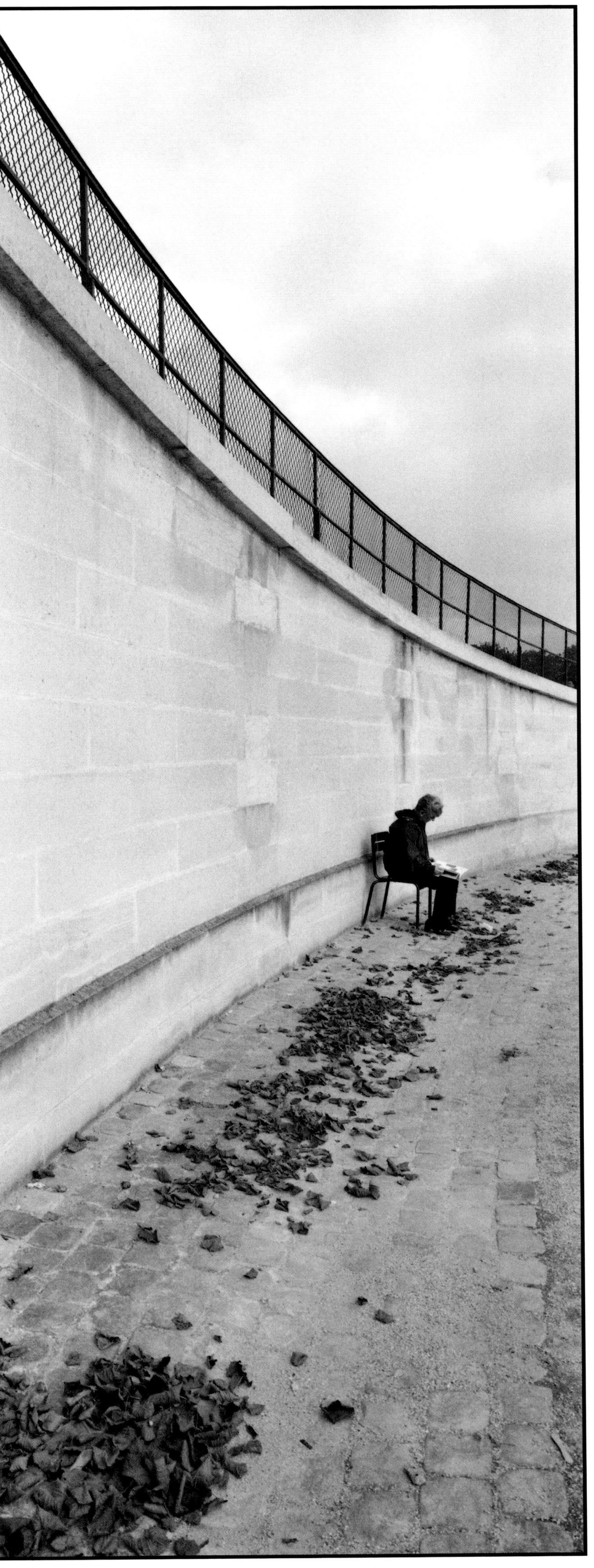

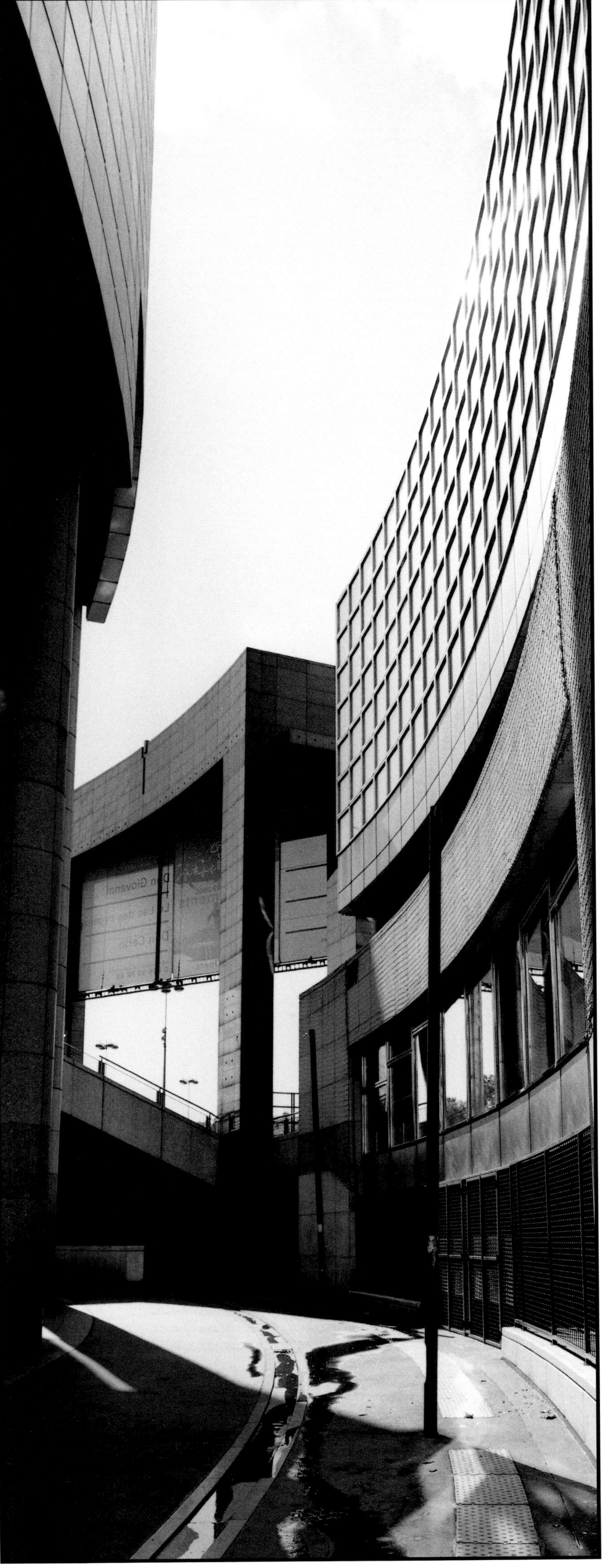

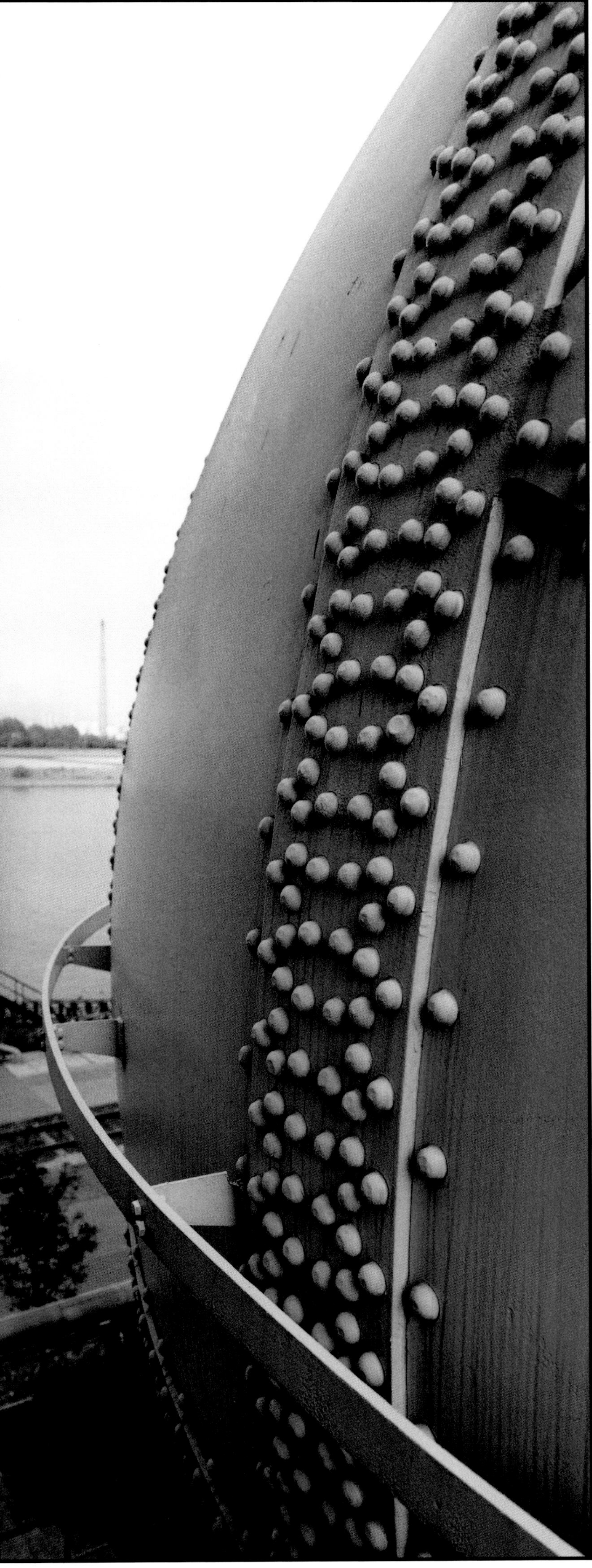

Industrial No. 103, Ludwigshafen / Rh. 1998

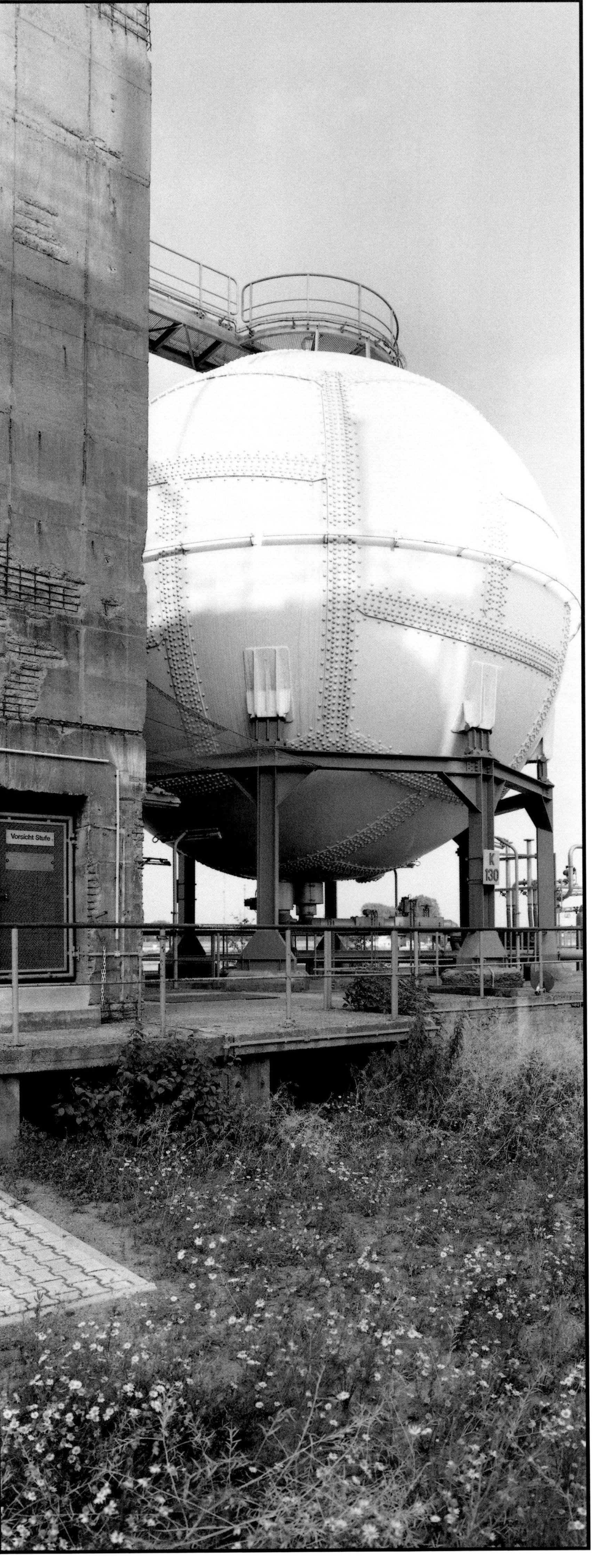

Vorsicht Stufe
K
130

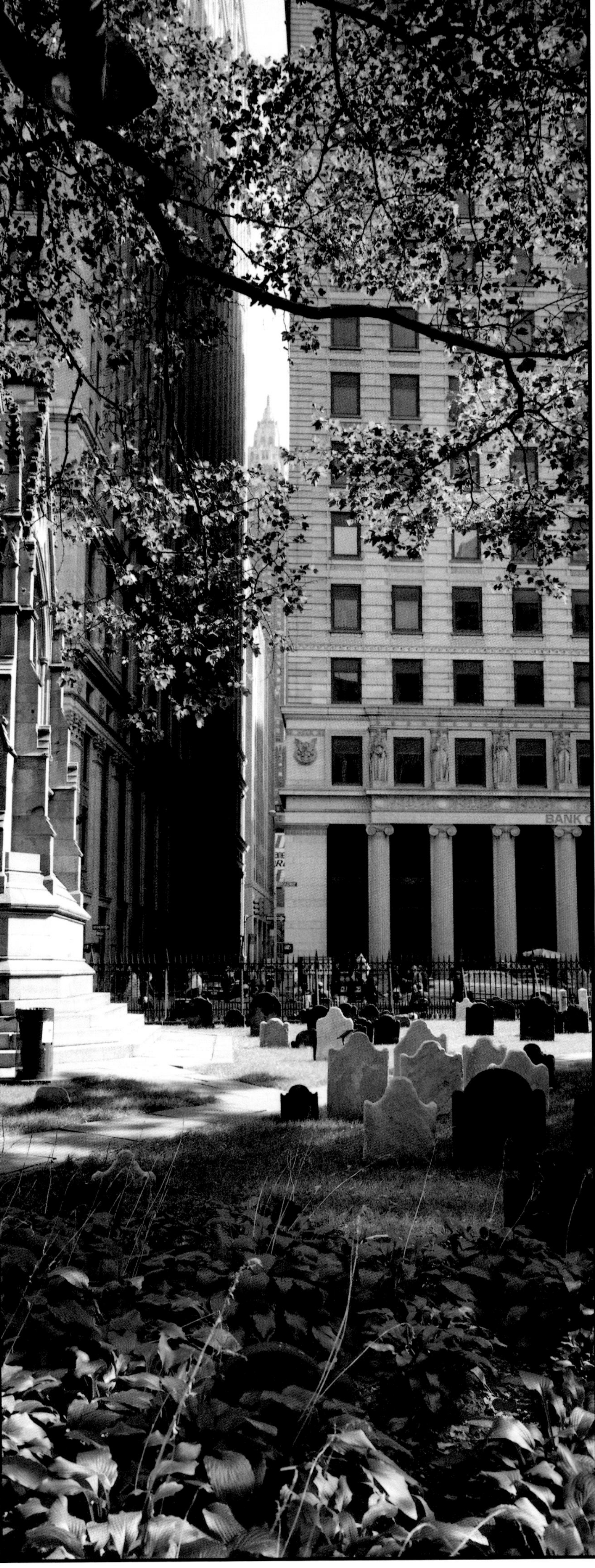

Nelson Tower, New York 1995

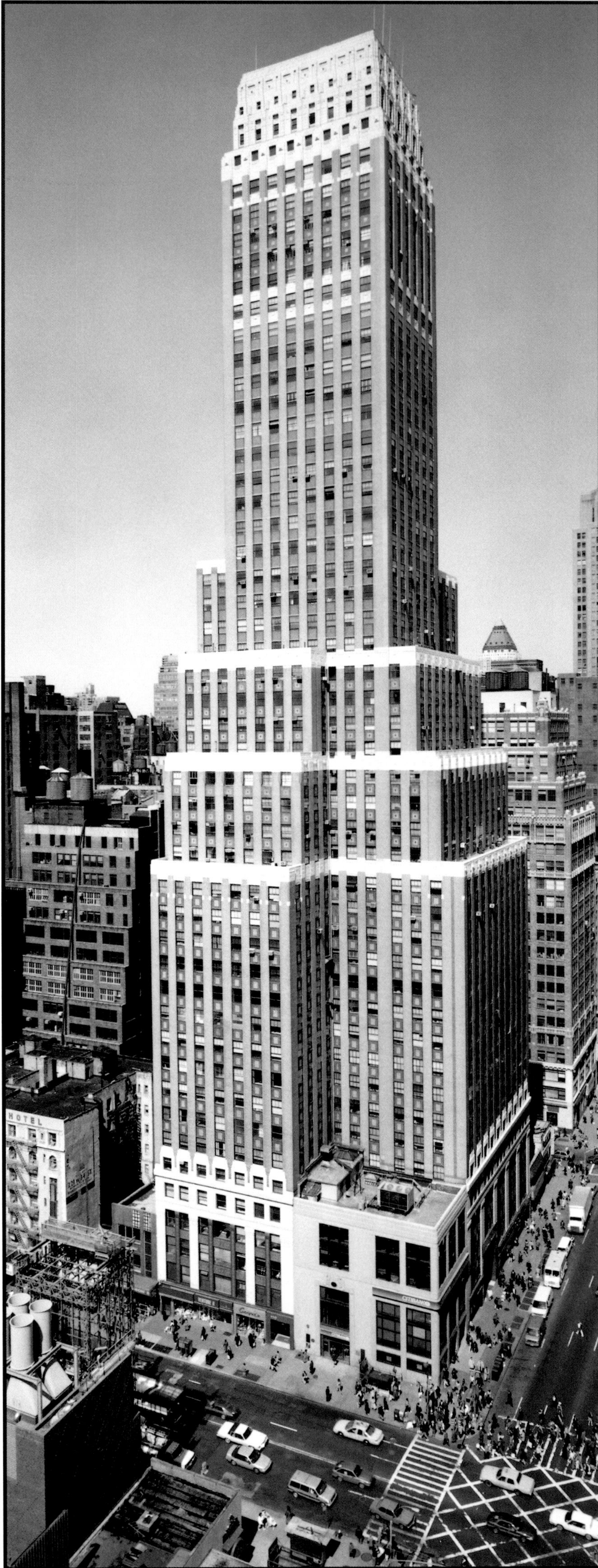

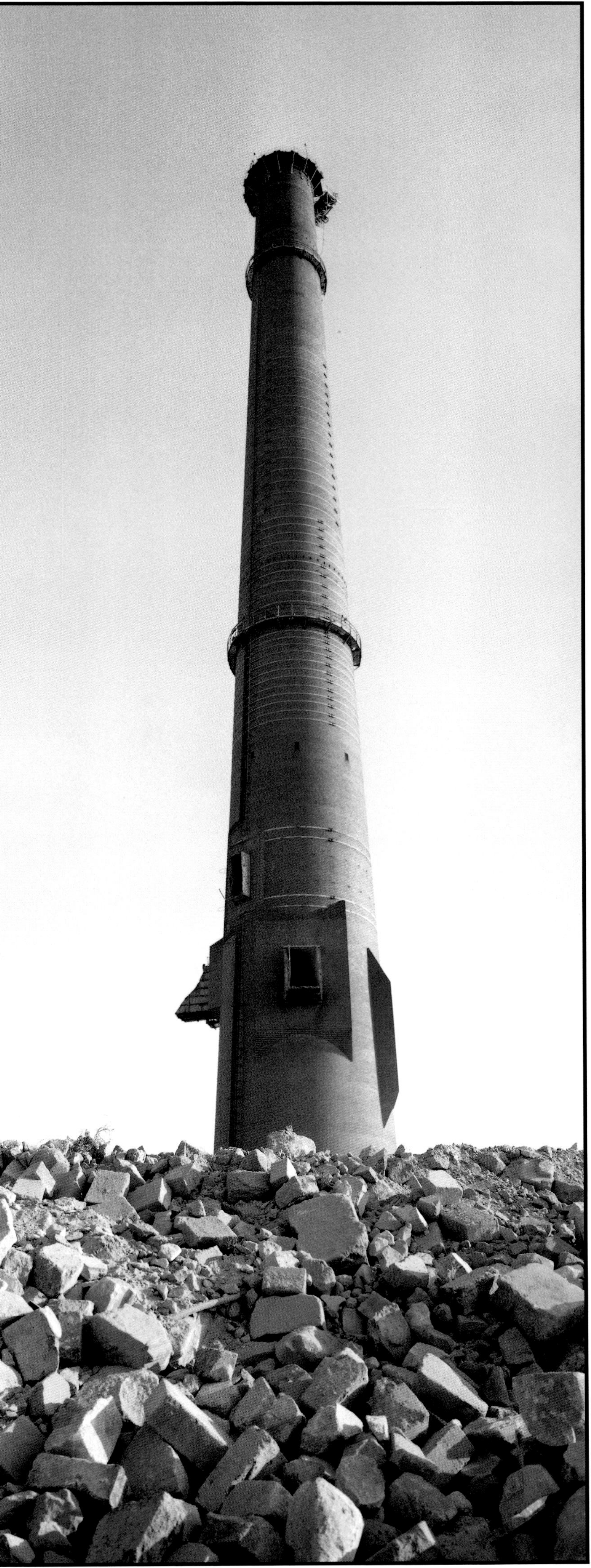

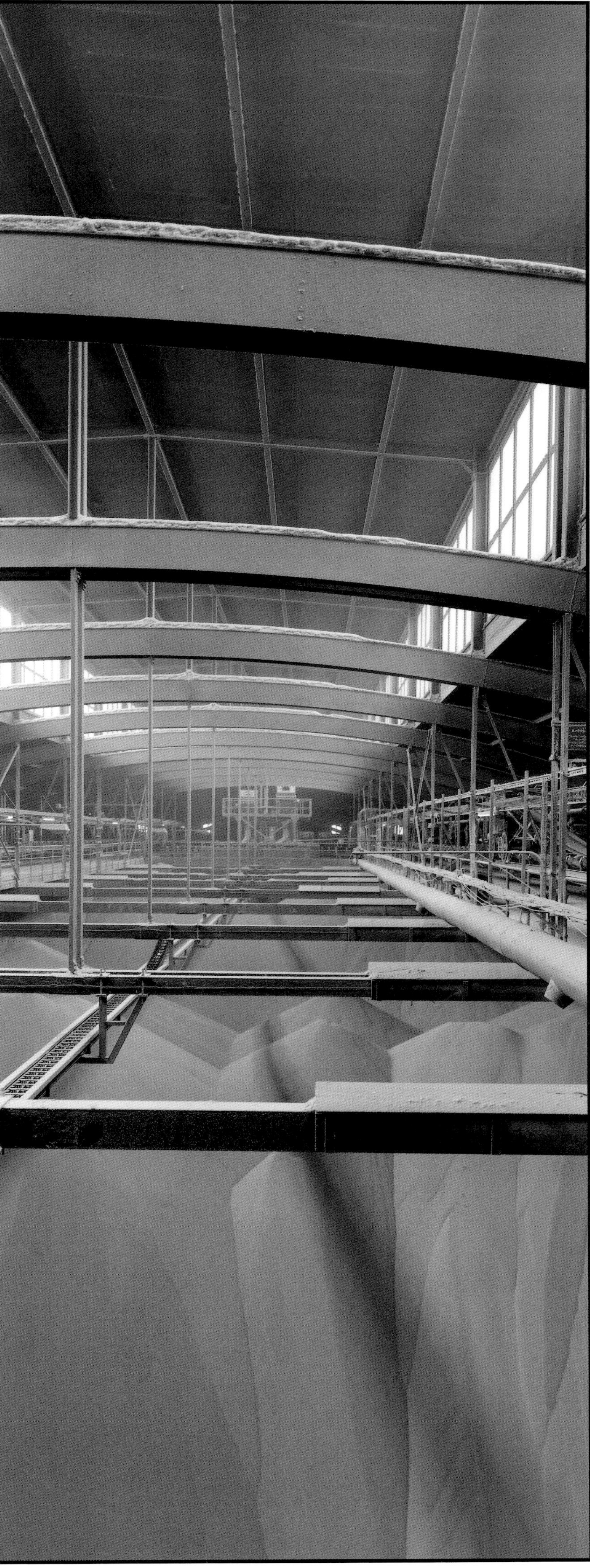

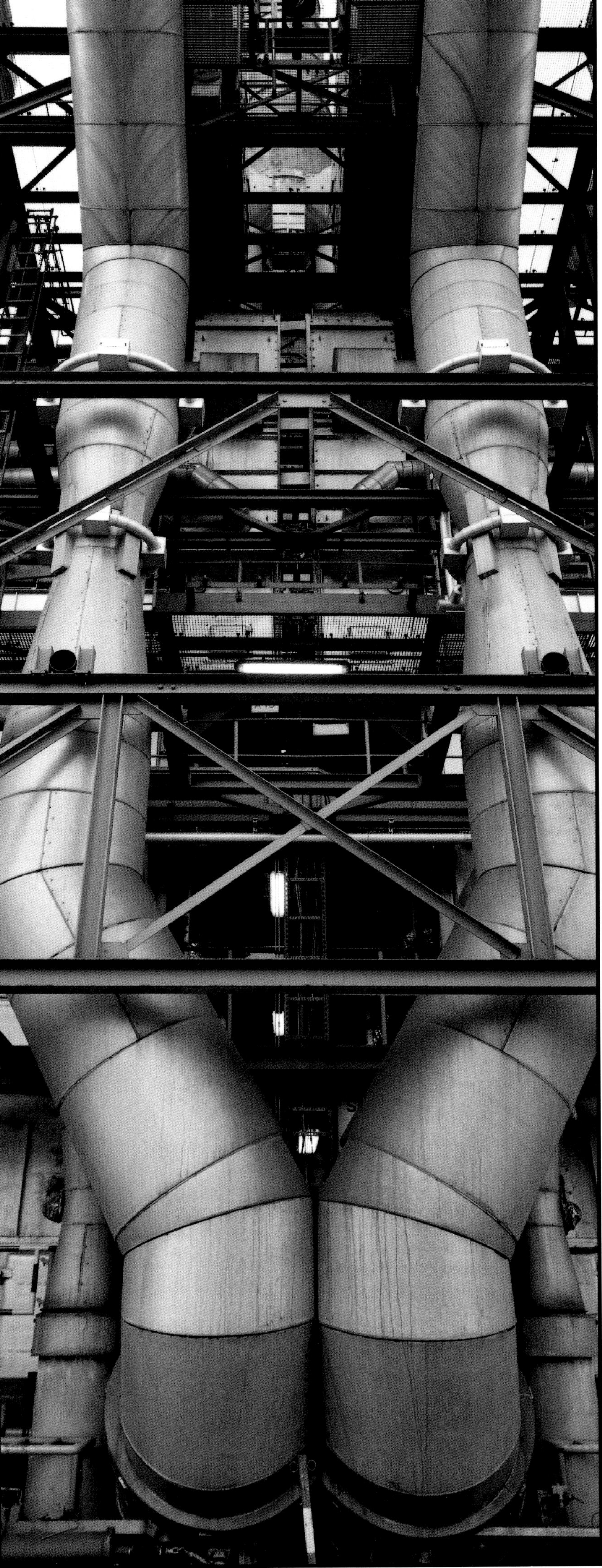

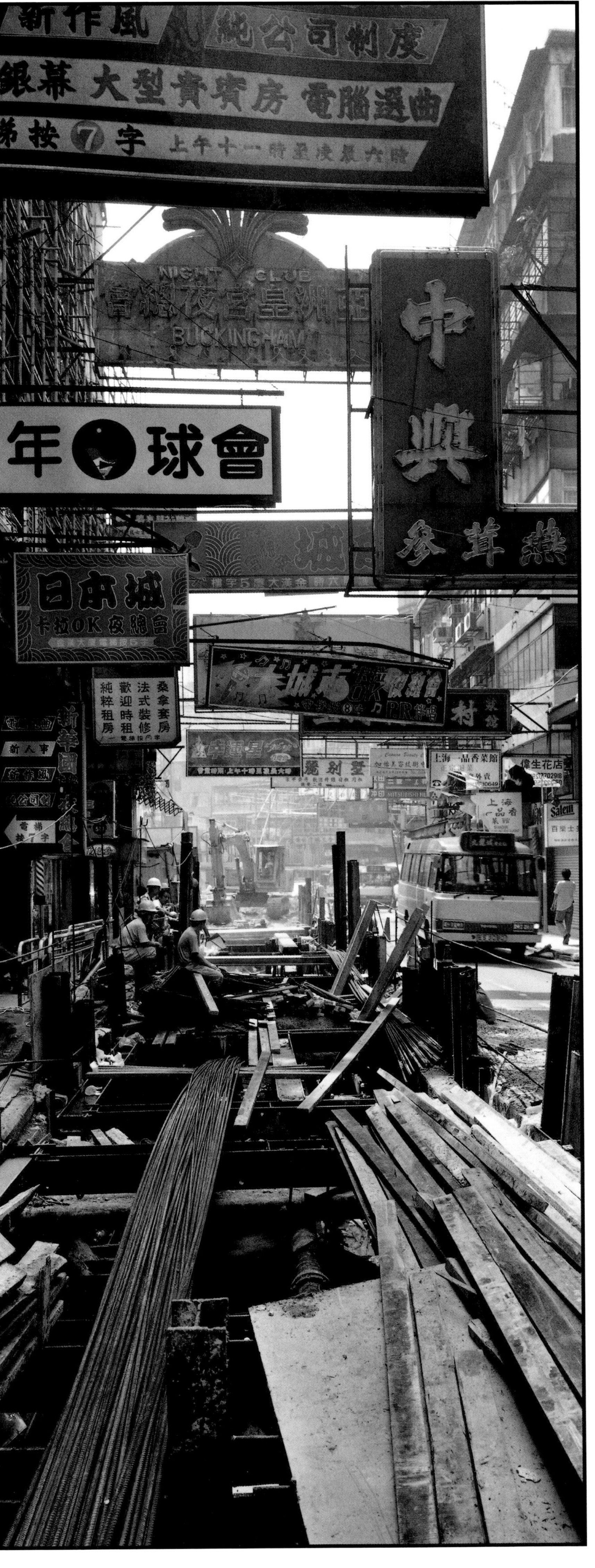
新作風
銀幕 大型貴賓房 電腦選曲
梯按 7 字 上午十一時至凌晨六陸
NIGHT CLUB
BUCKINGHAM
夜總會
青年 球會
中興
日本城
卡拉OK夜總會
參茸藥
上海一品香菜館

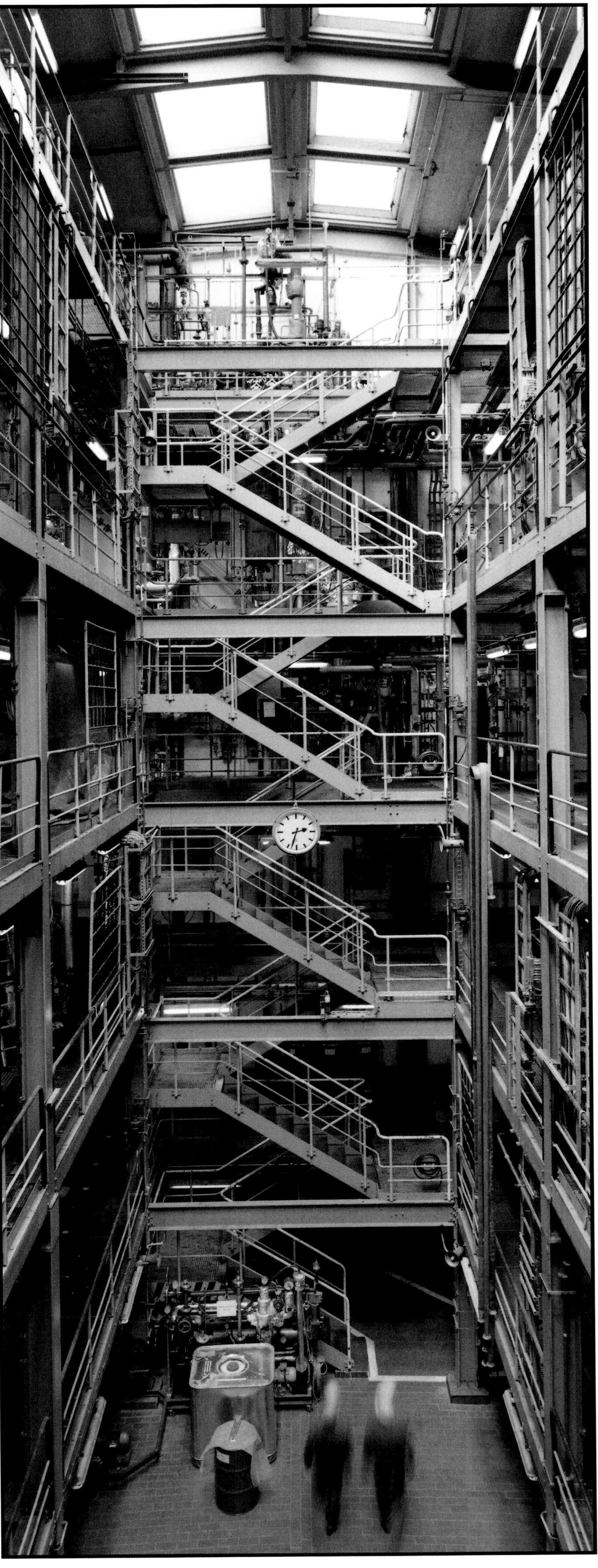

Bank of China, Hong Kong 1996

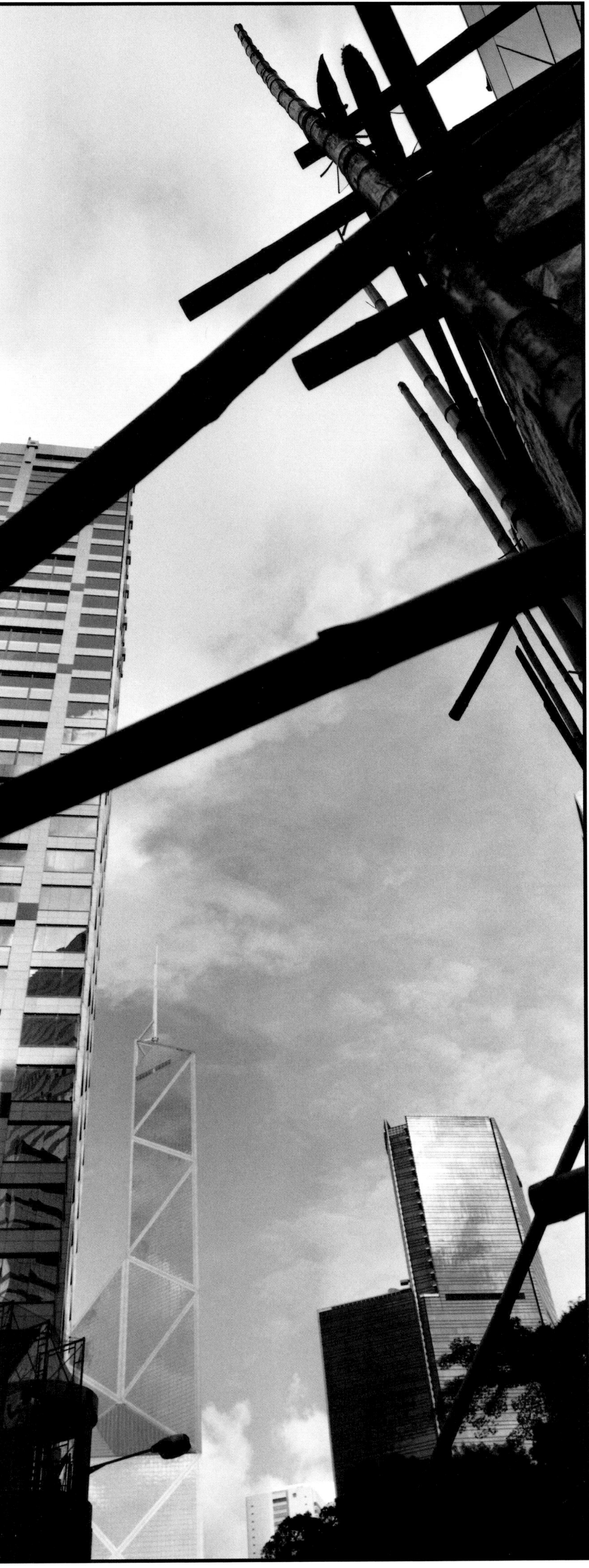

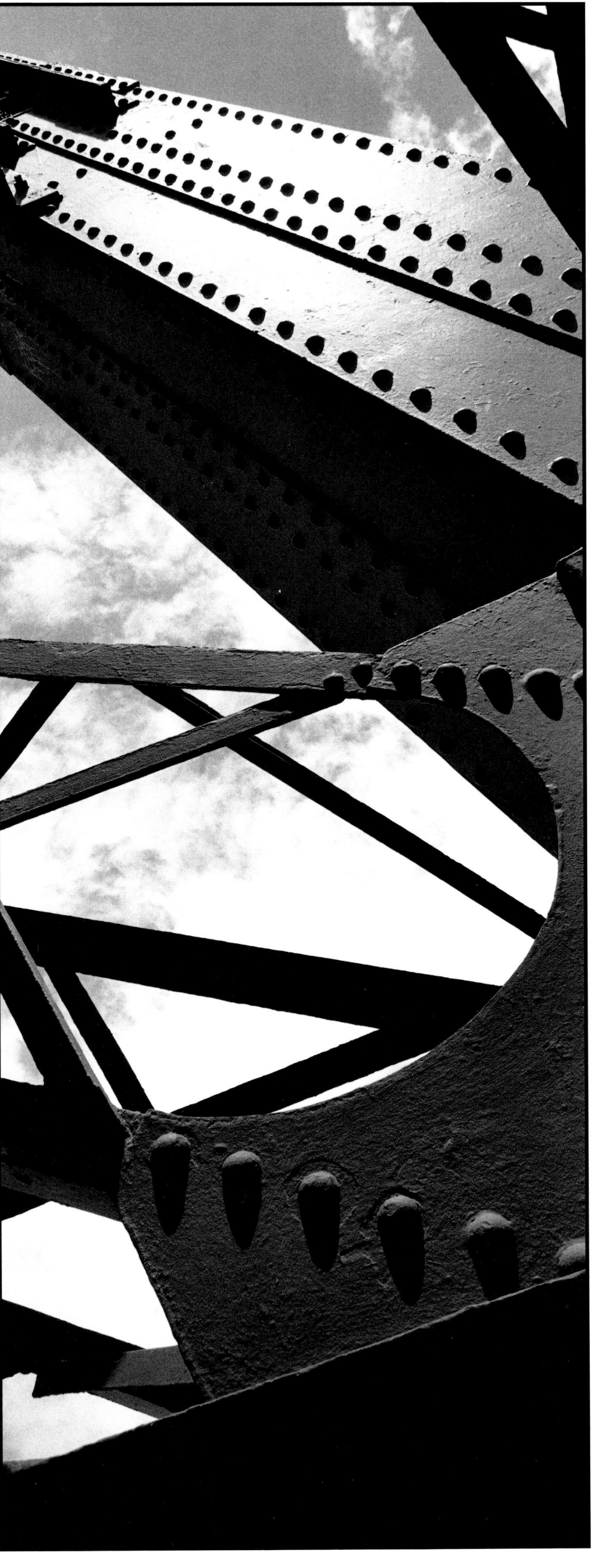

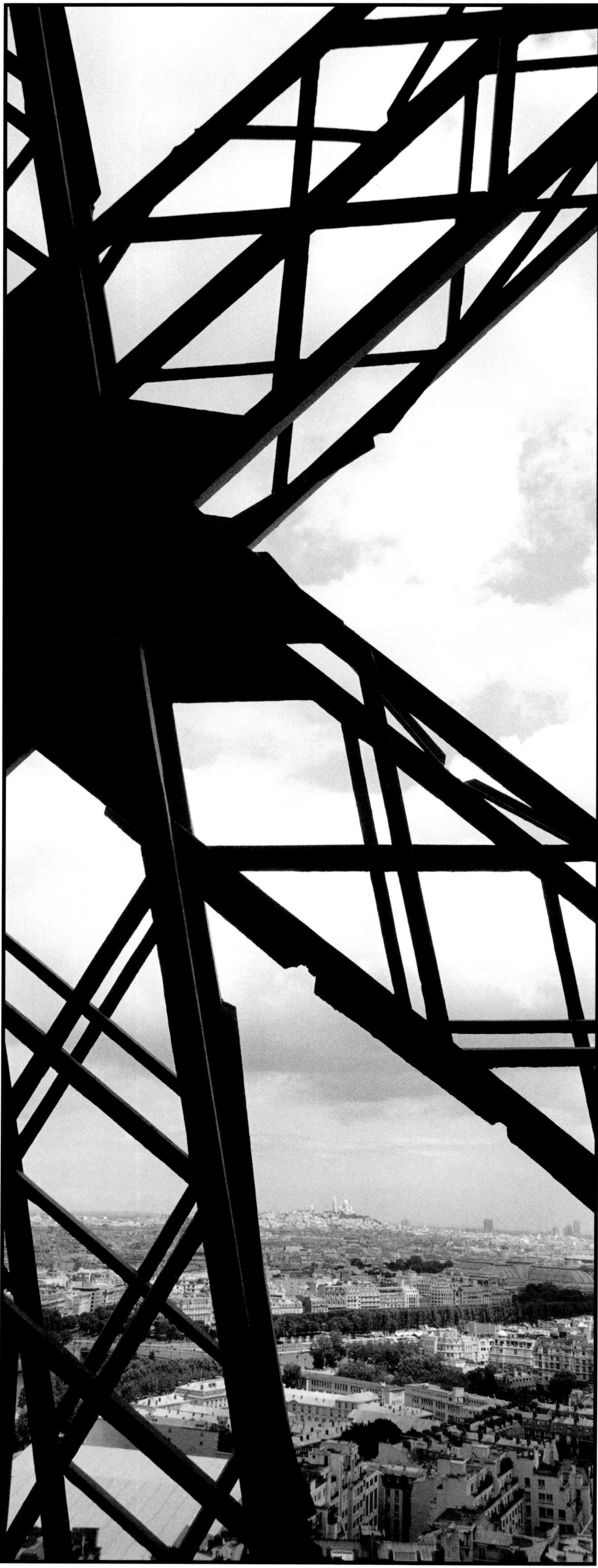

Tour Eiffel, Montmartre, Paris 1999

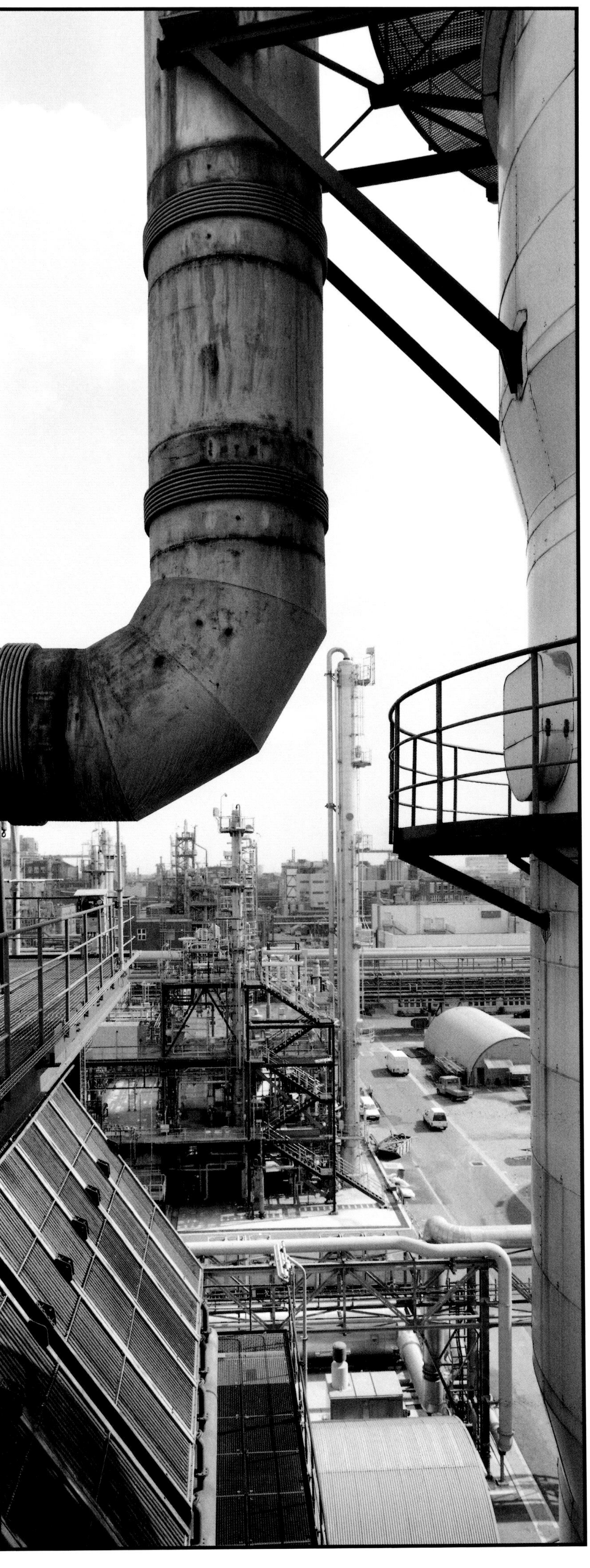

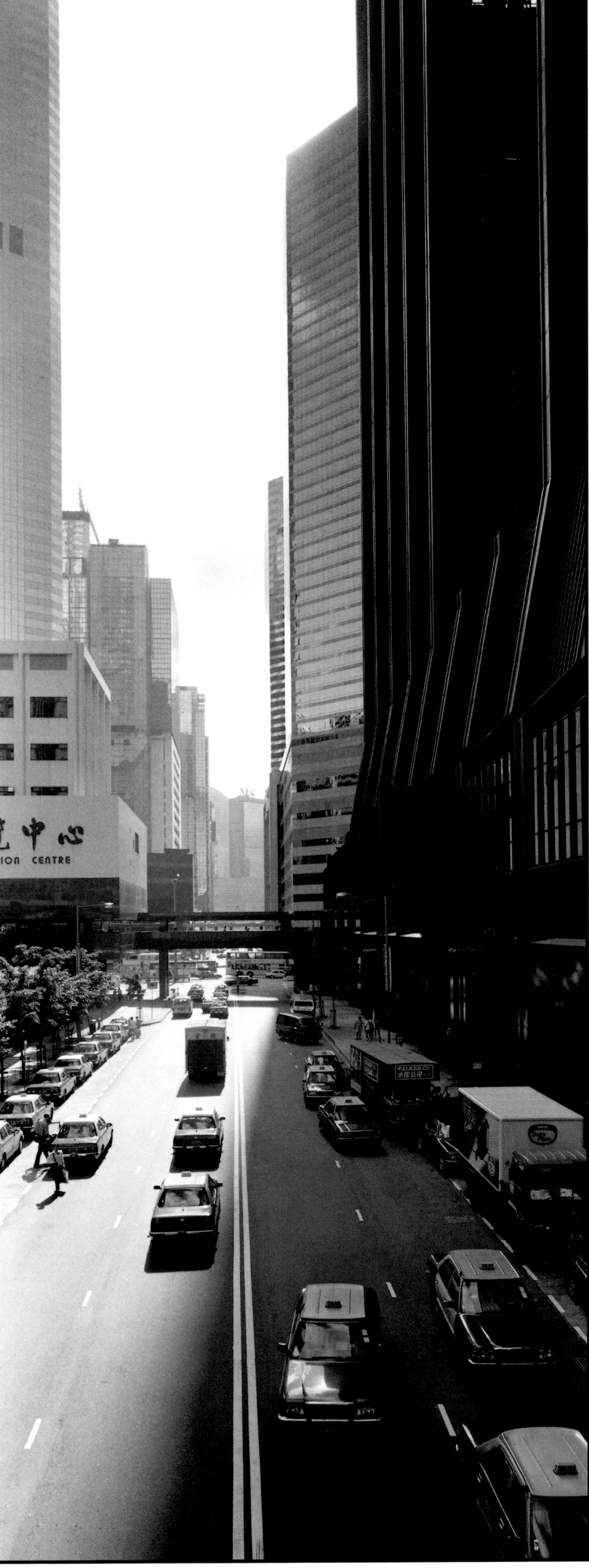

Montgomery Street, San Francisco 2000

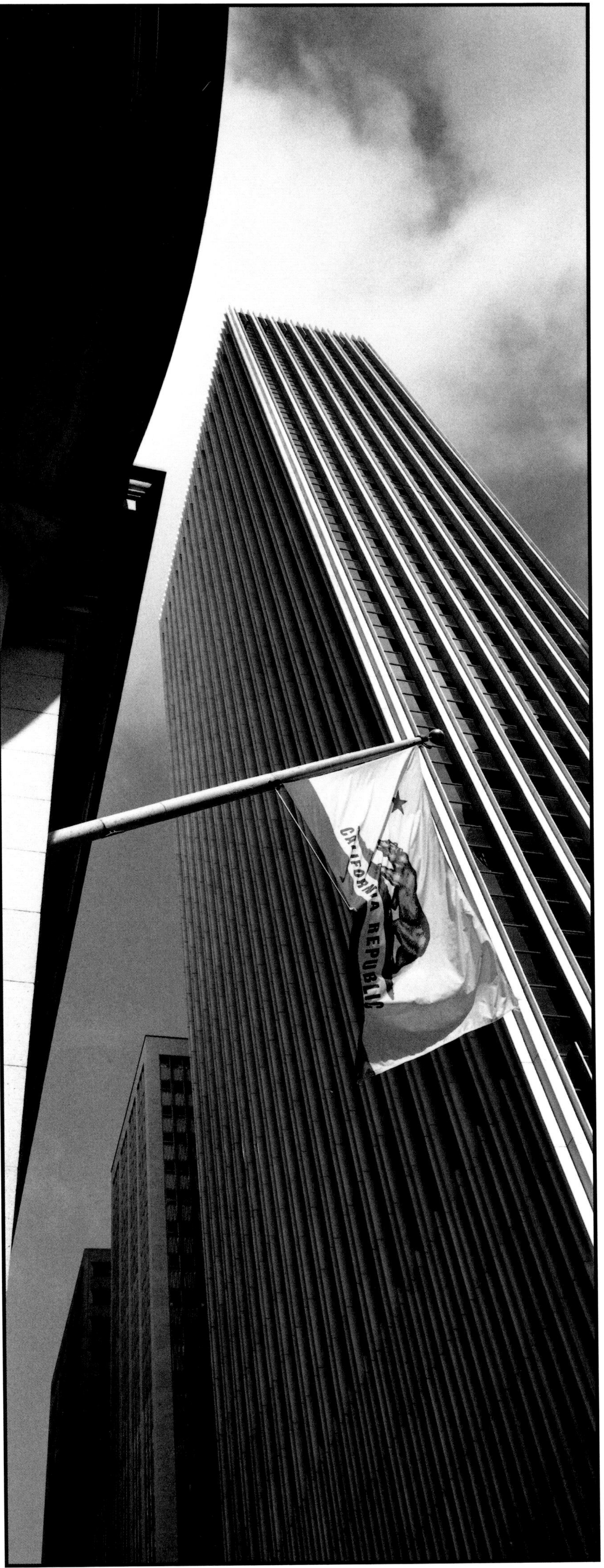
CALIFORNIA REPUBLIC

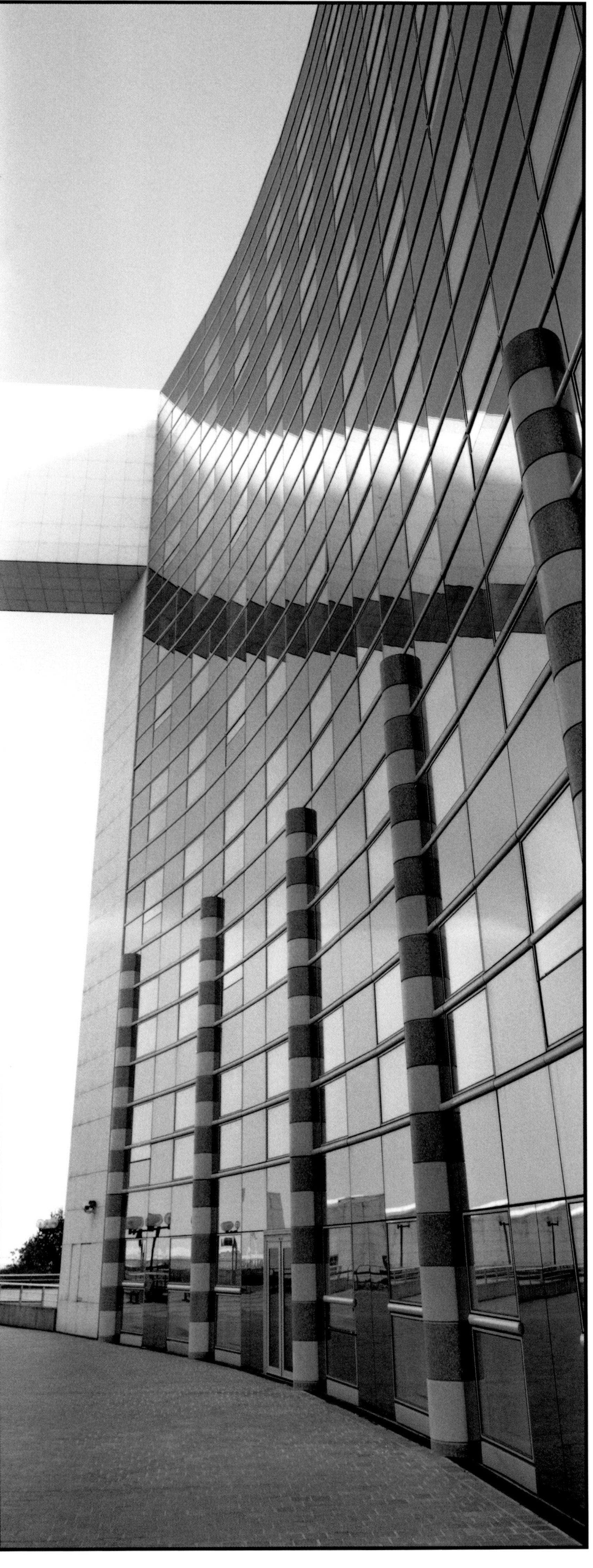

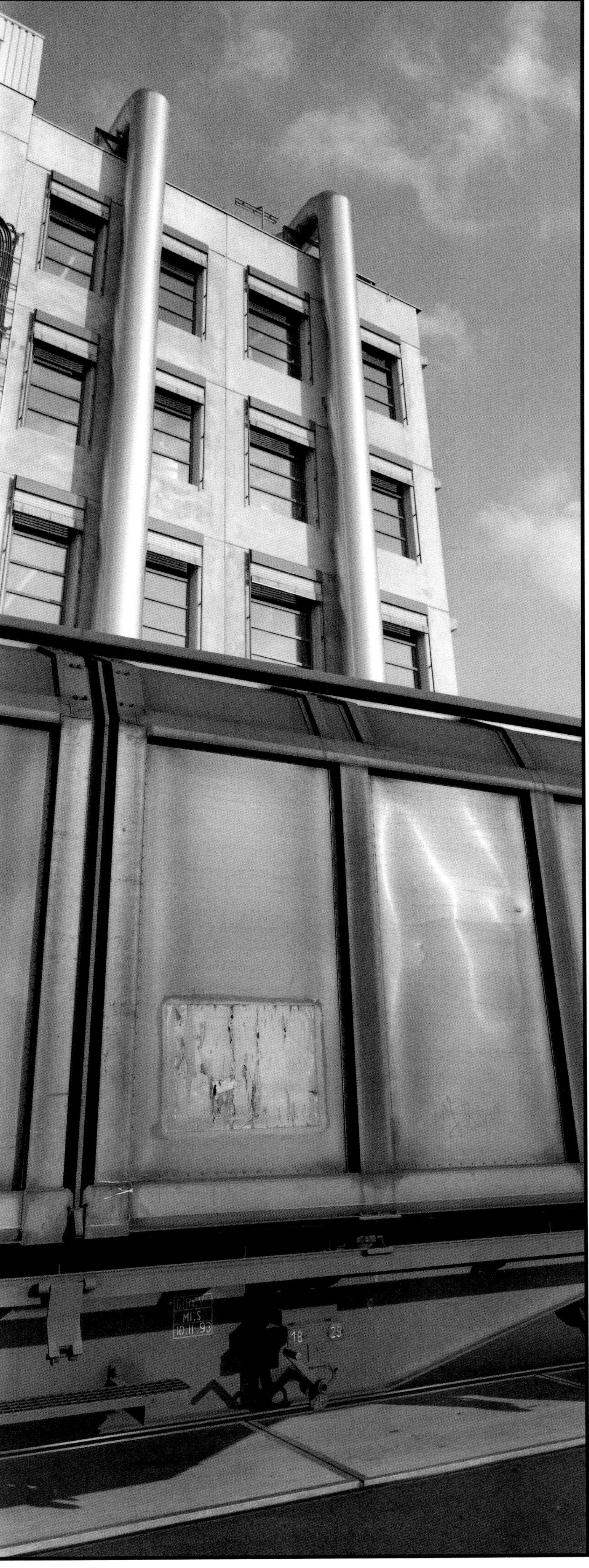

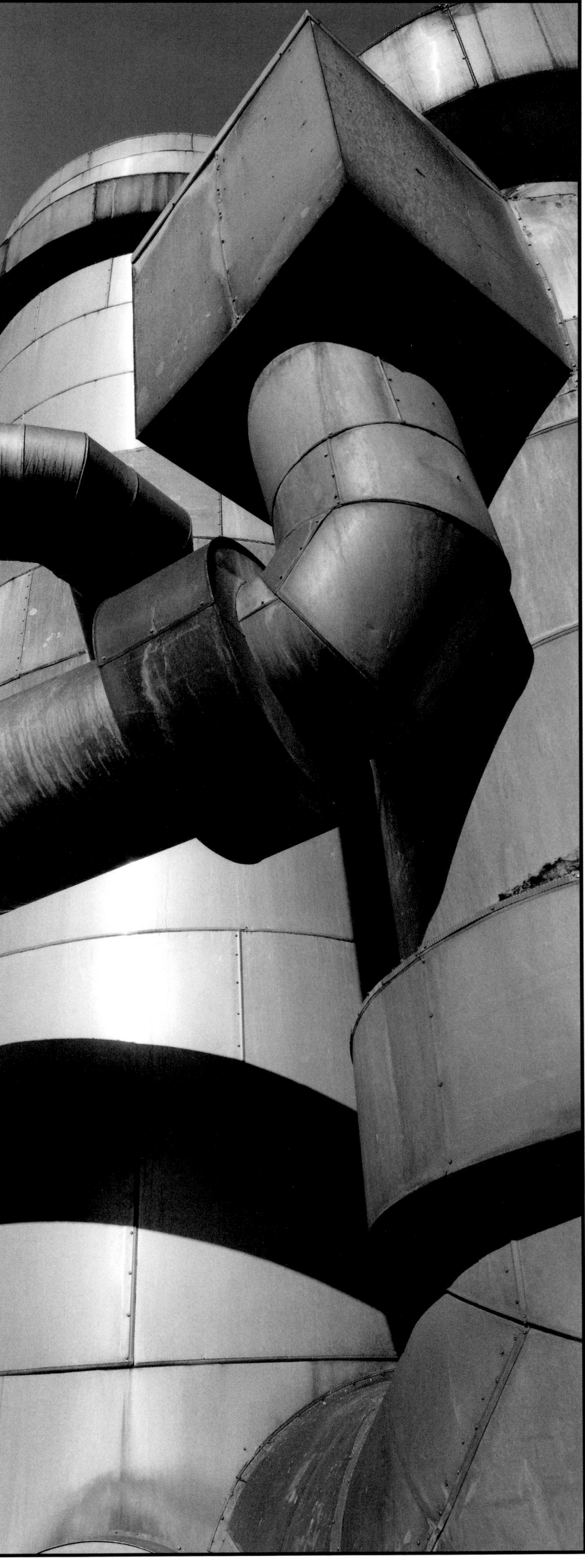

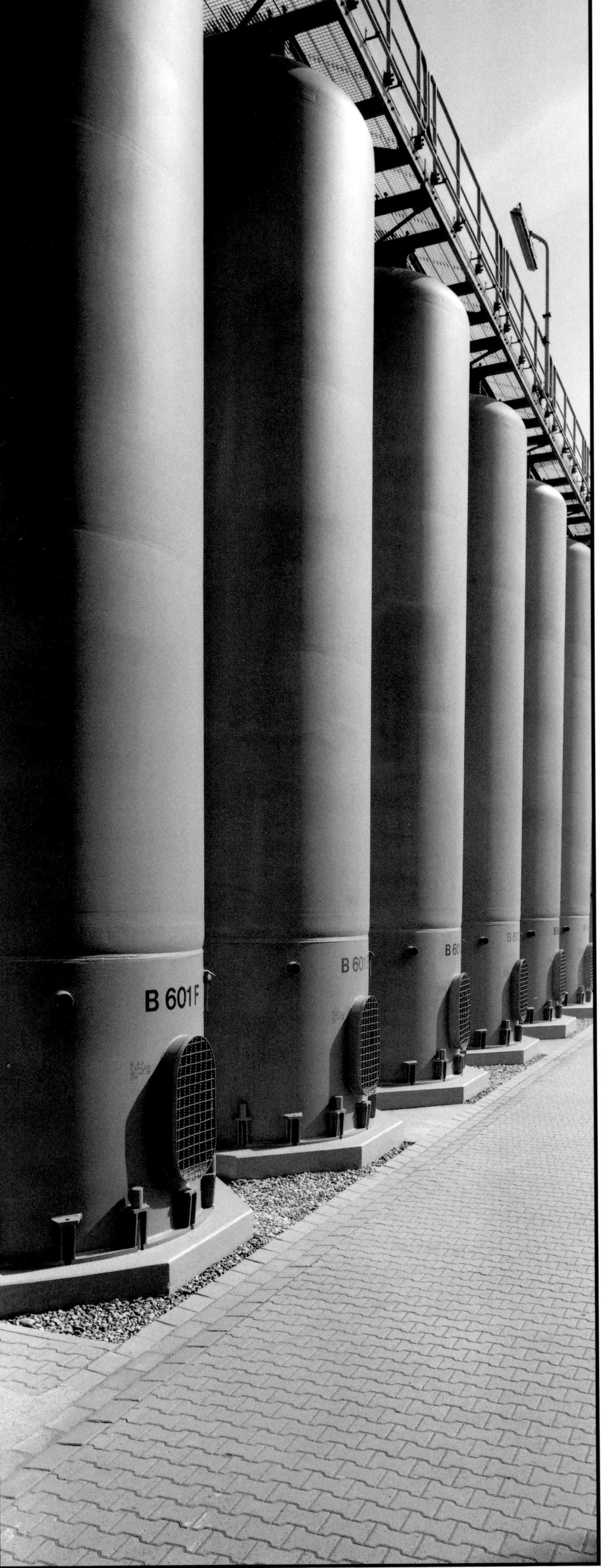

B 601F
B 601
B 60

Grand Palais, Paris 1998

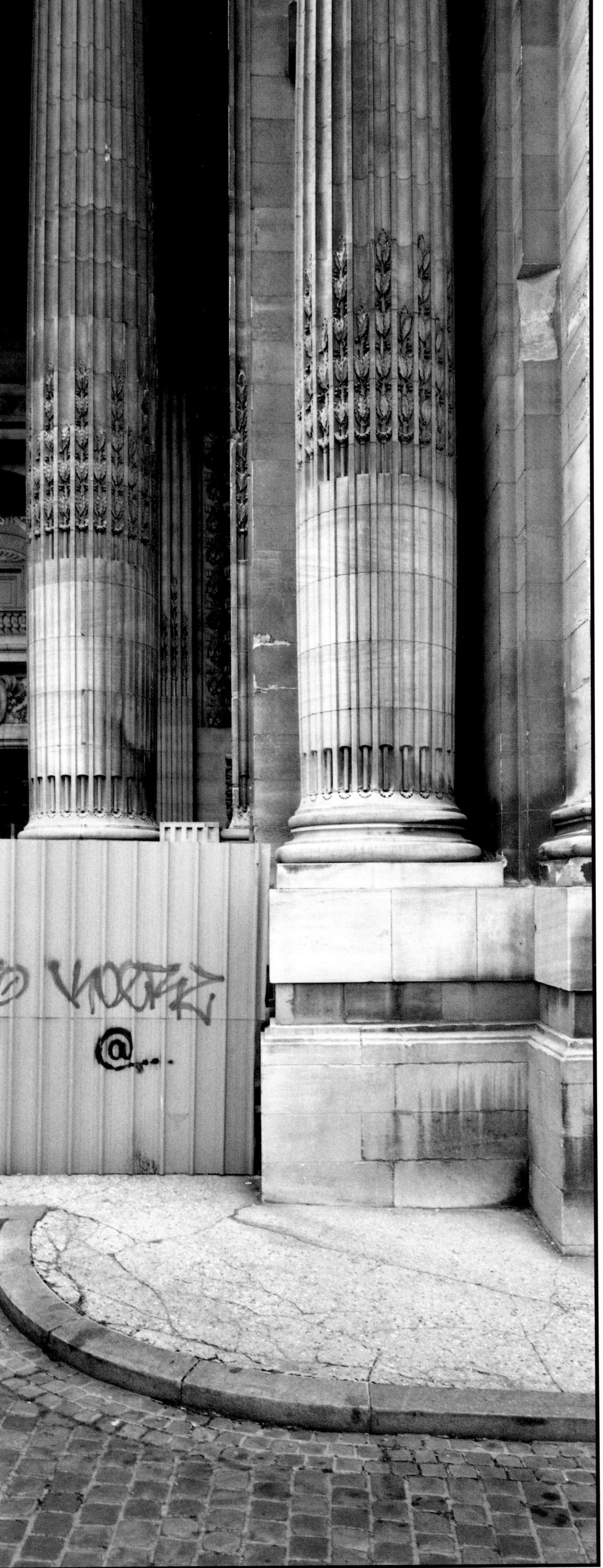

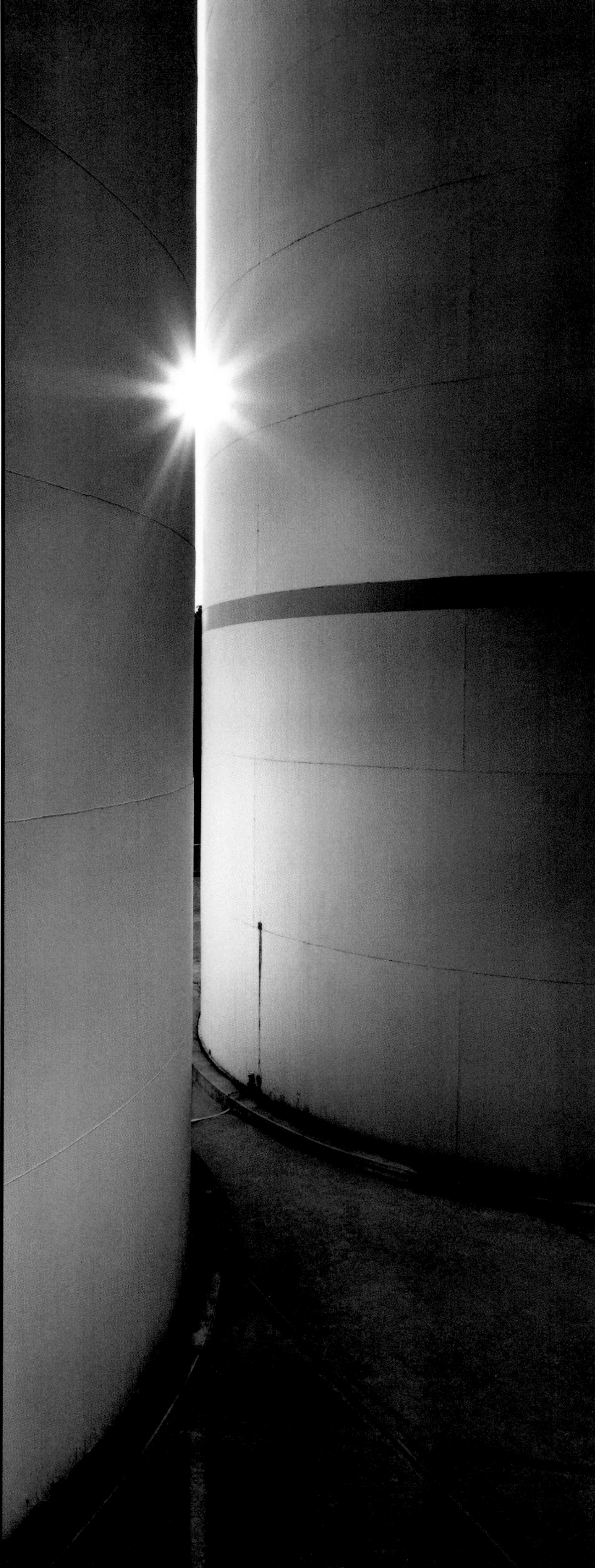

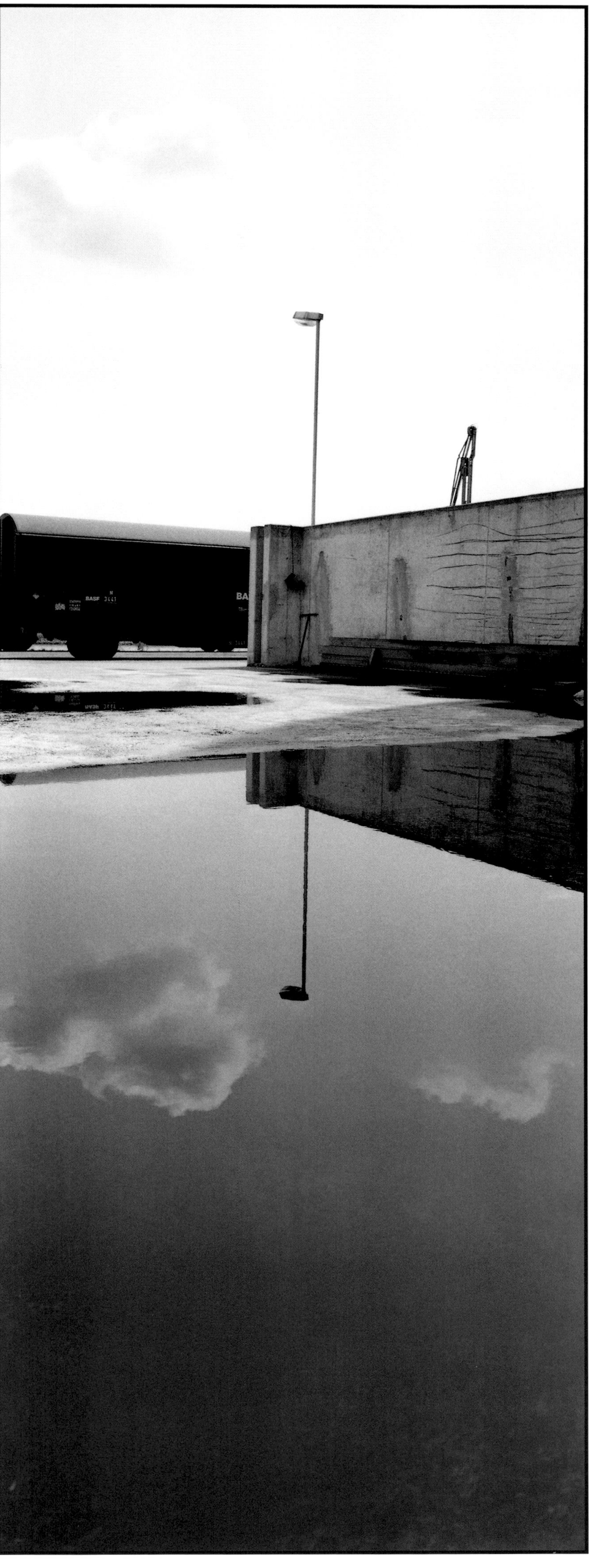

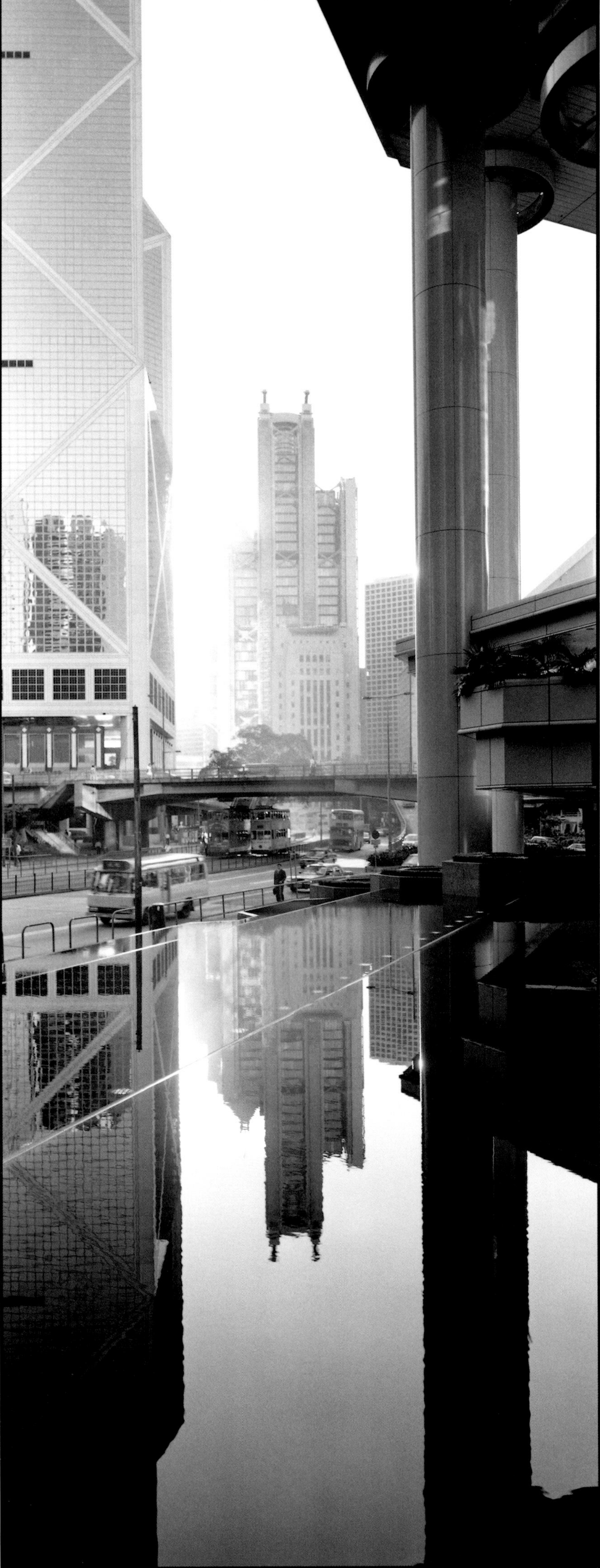

Victoria Peak II, Hong Kong 1996

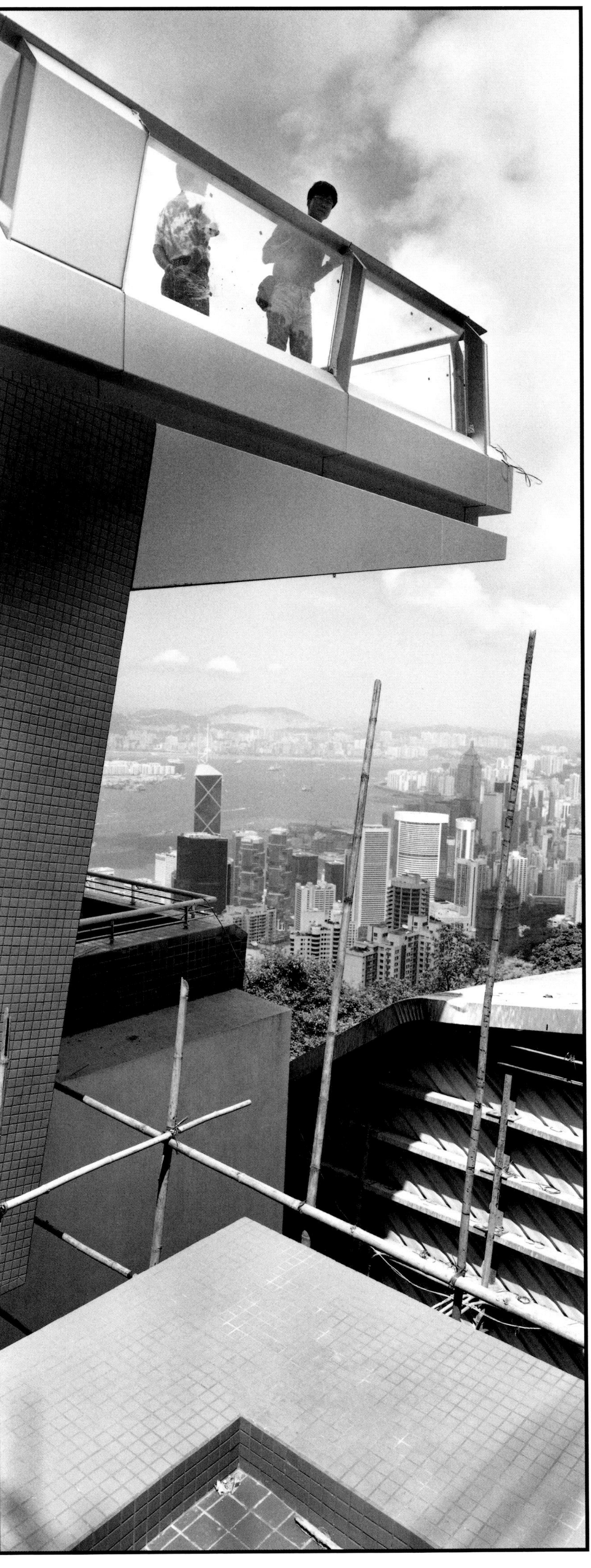

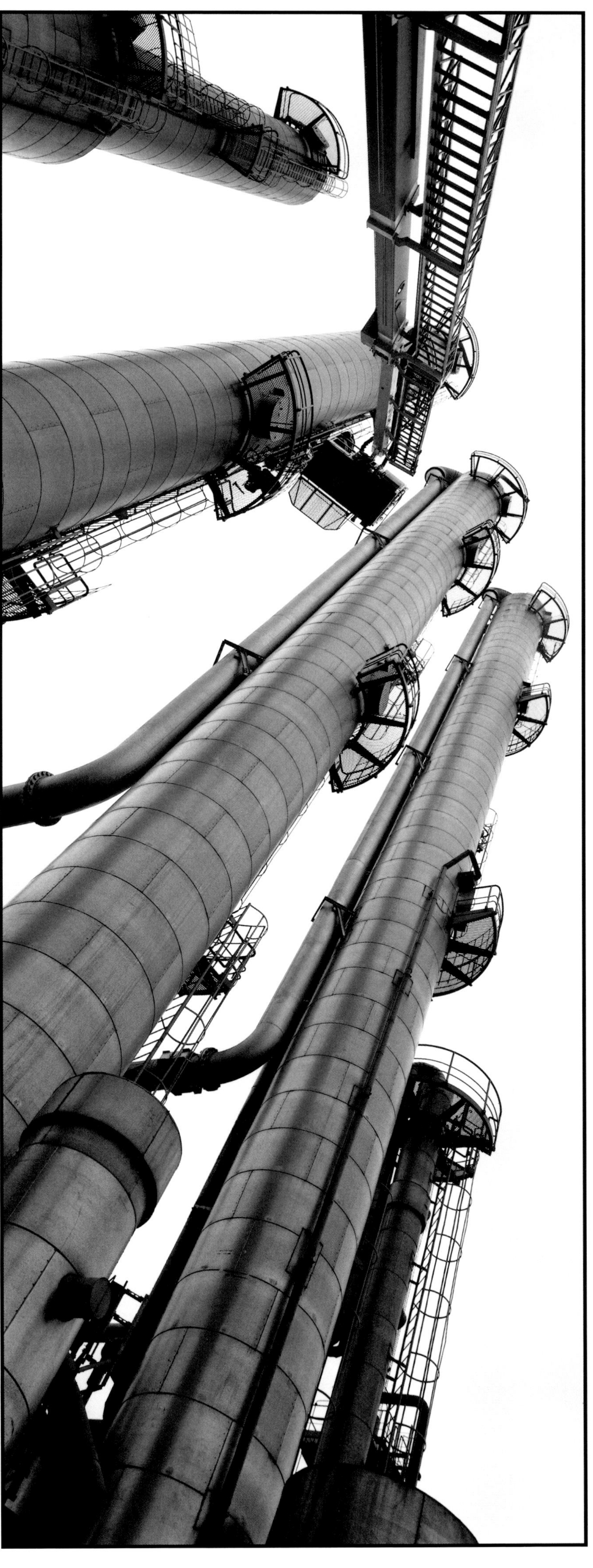

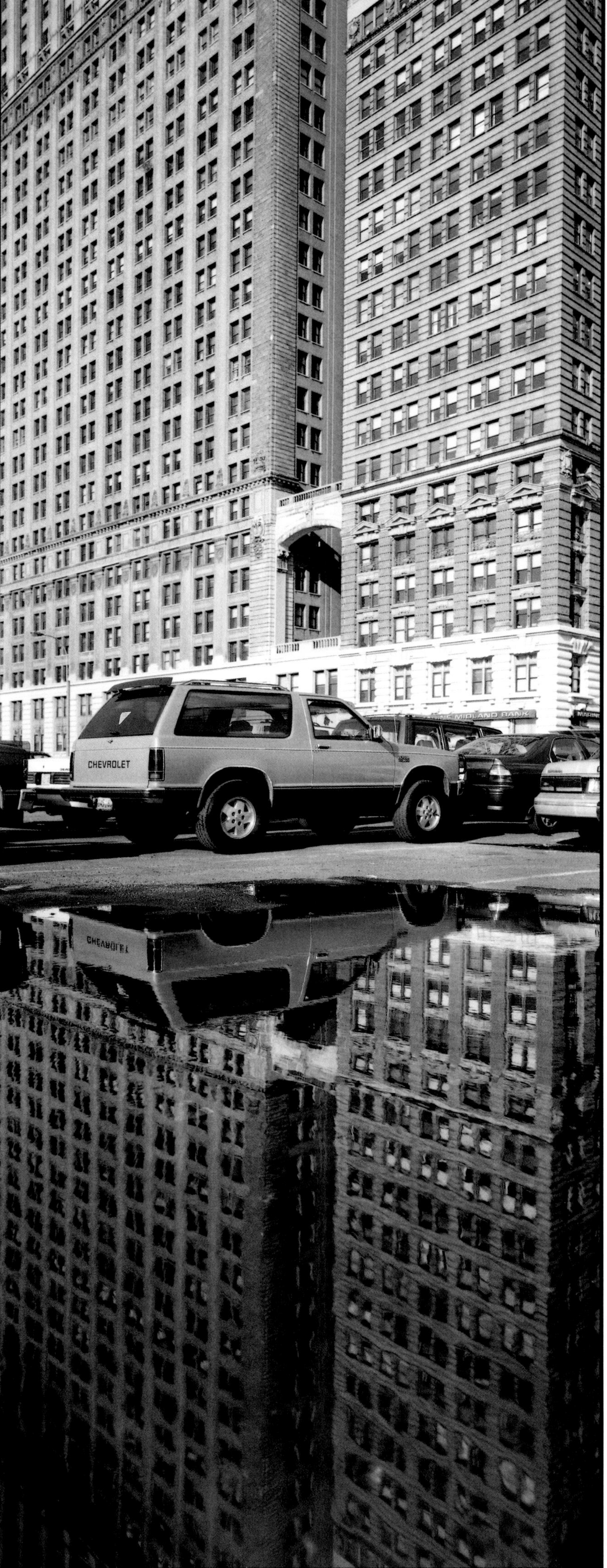
CHEVROLET

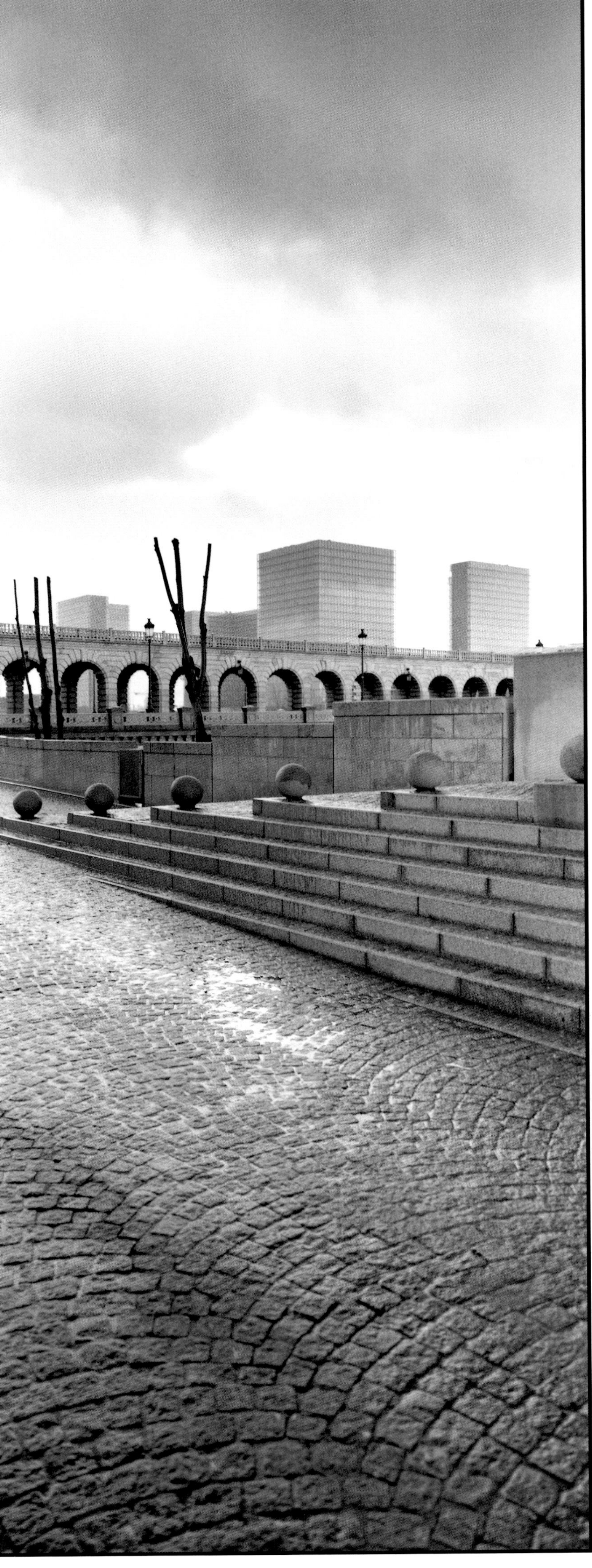

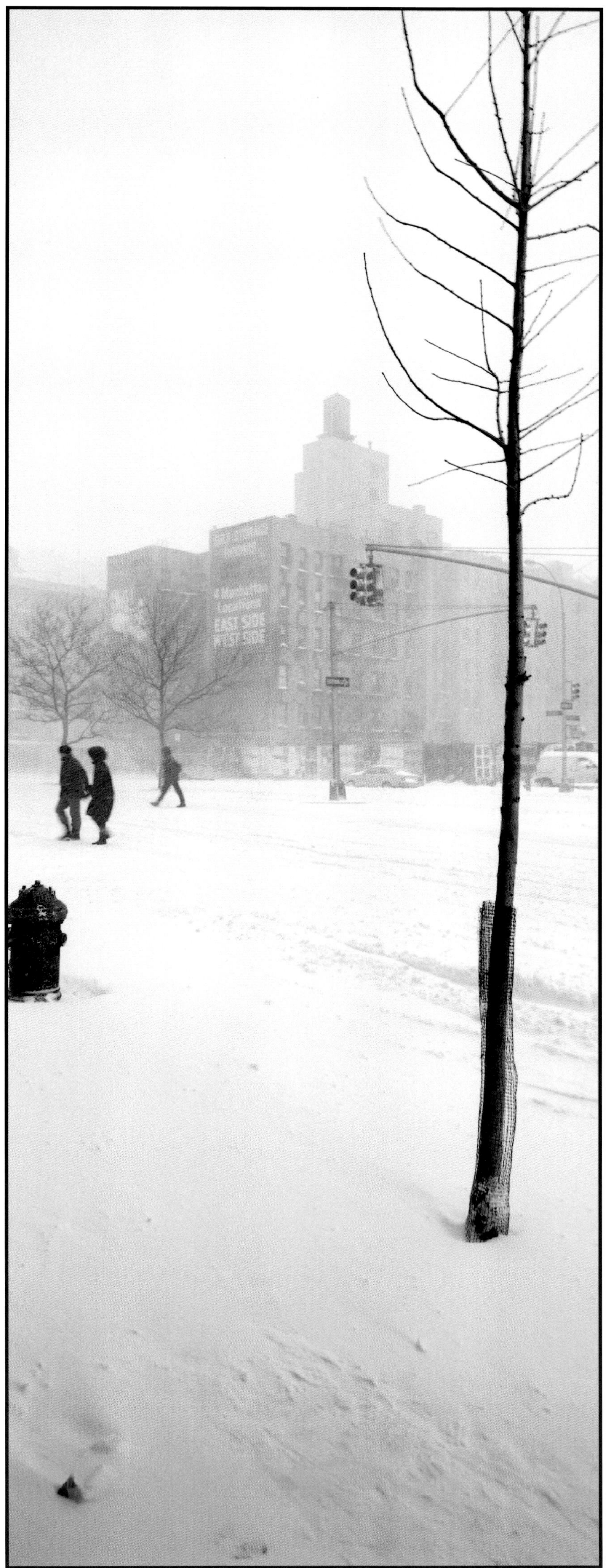
4 Manhattan
Locations
EAST SIDE
WEST SIDE

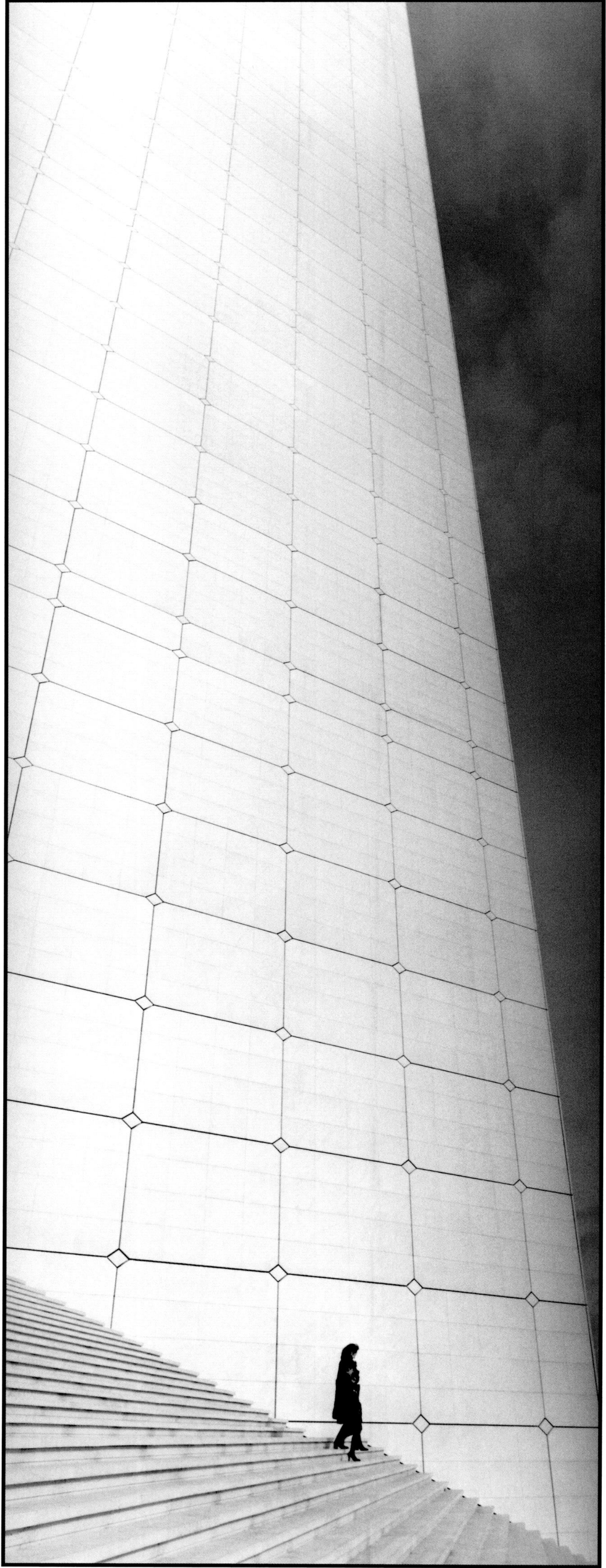

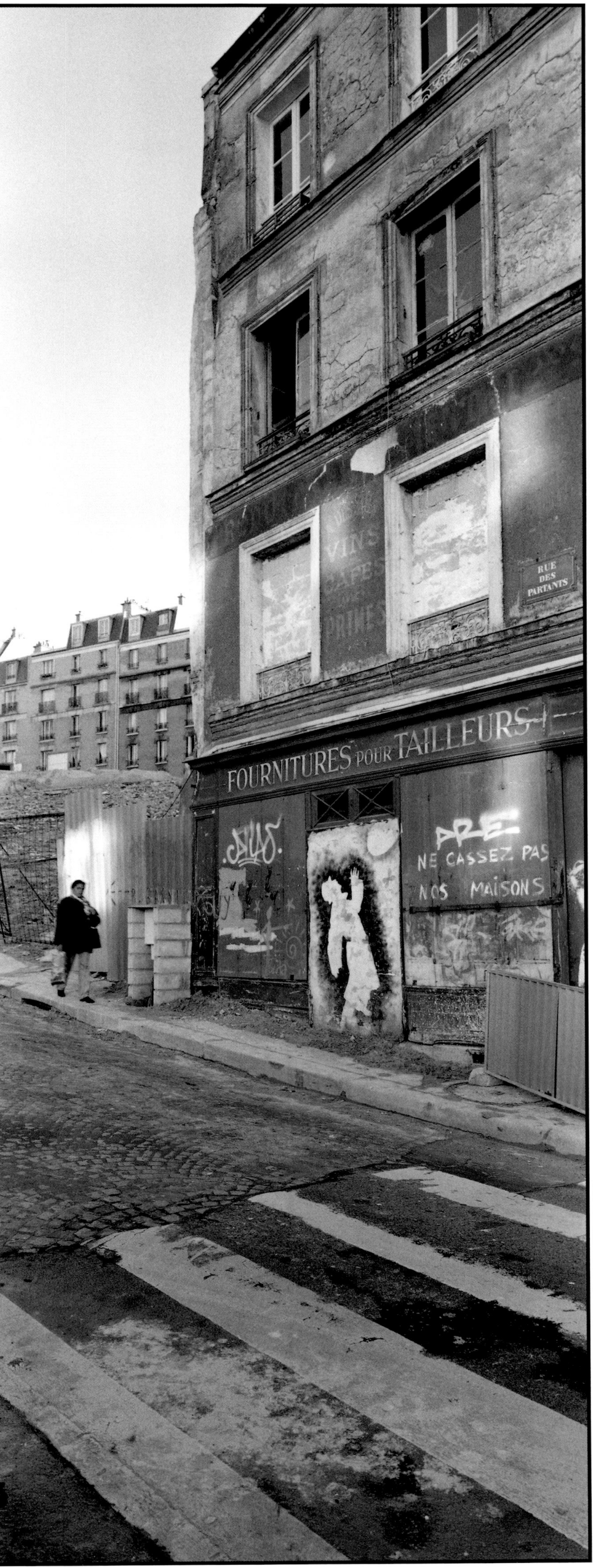
RUE
DES
PARTANTS
VINS
PRIN
FOURNITURES POUR TAILLEURS
PRE
NE CASSEZ PAS
NOS MAISONS

Quim Cardona, New York 2001

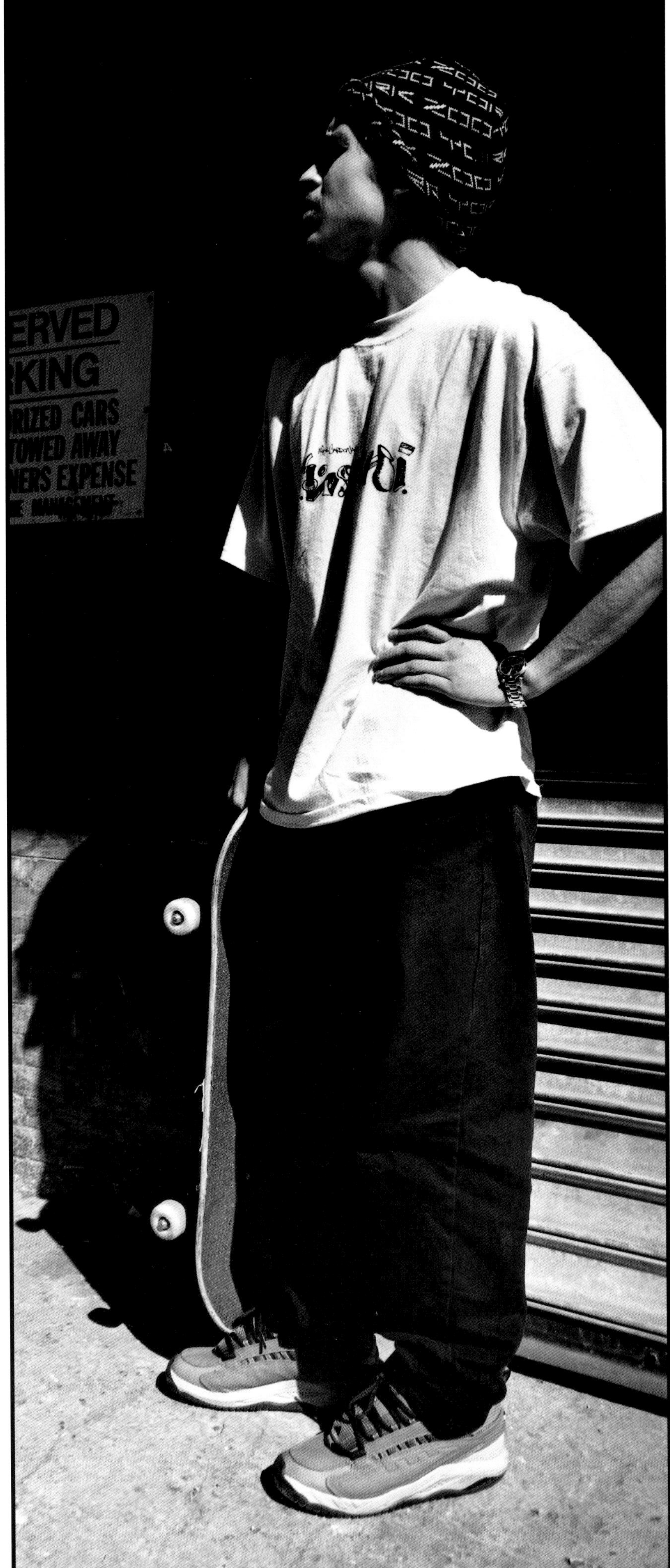

ERVED
RKING
RIZED CARS
TOWED AWAY
NERS EXPENSE
E MANAGEMENT

Dany Supa, New York 2001

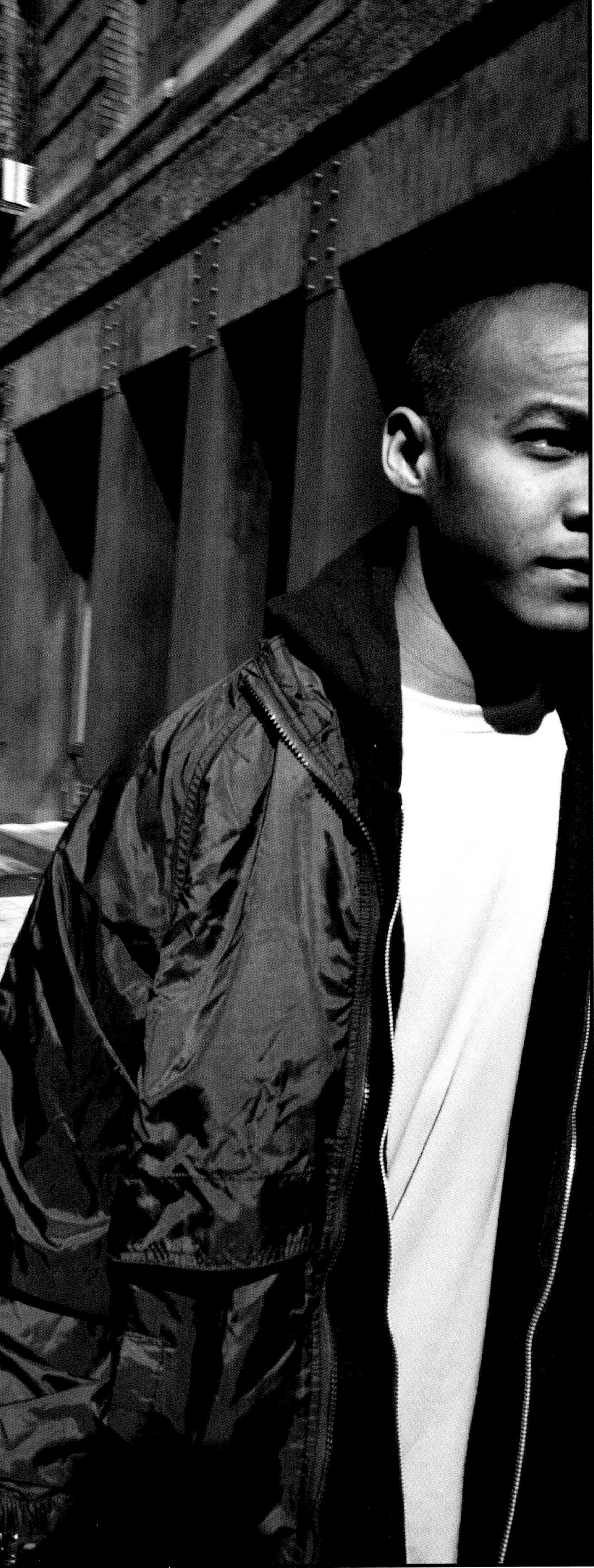

La Défense II, Paris 1997

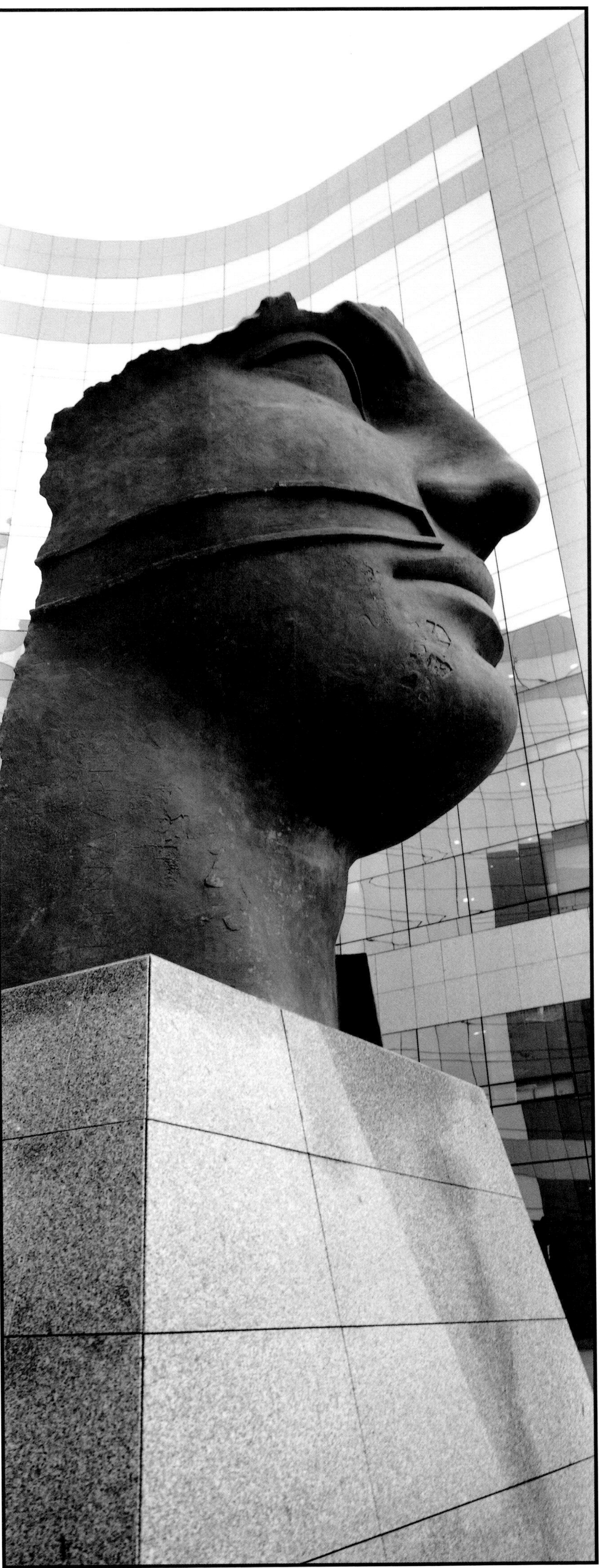

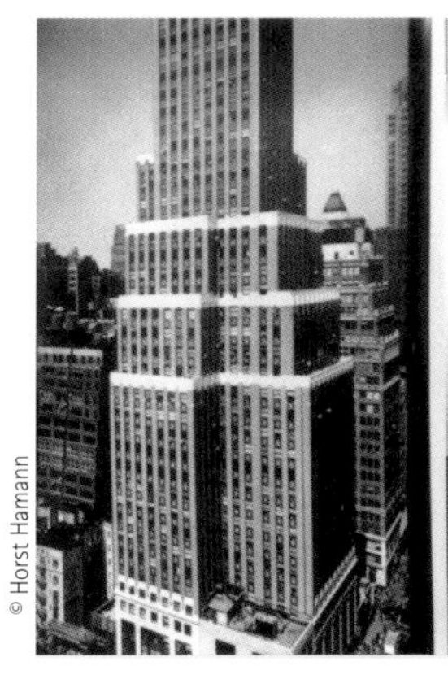
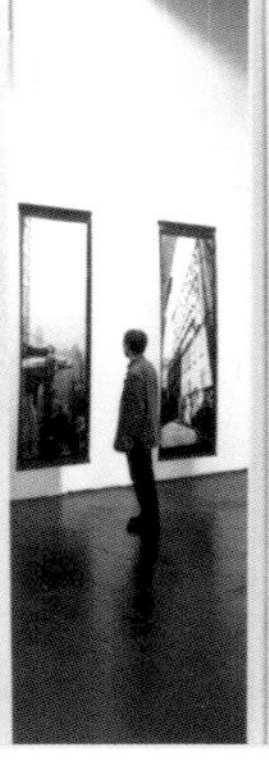
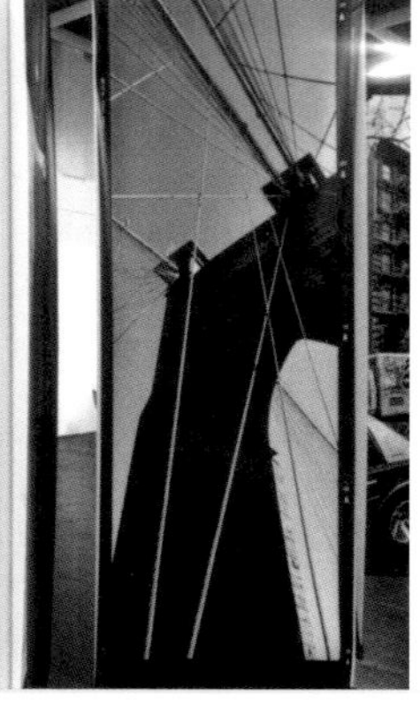

New York Vertical Book Lounge and Exhibition
Photokina, Cologne

Photographer Horst Hamann with text author Volker Skierka
Photokina, Cologne

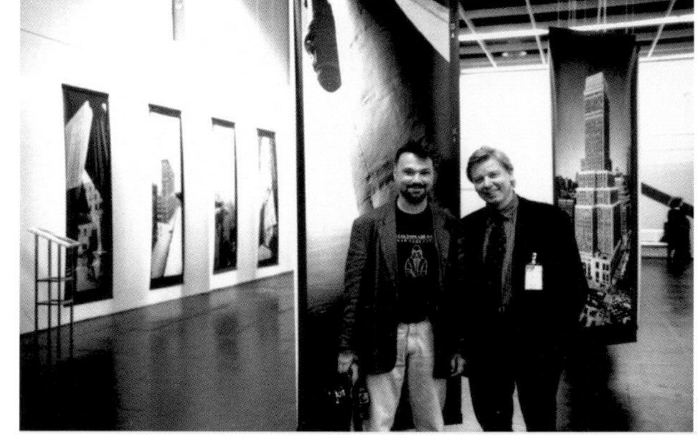

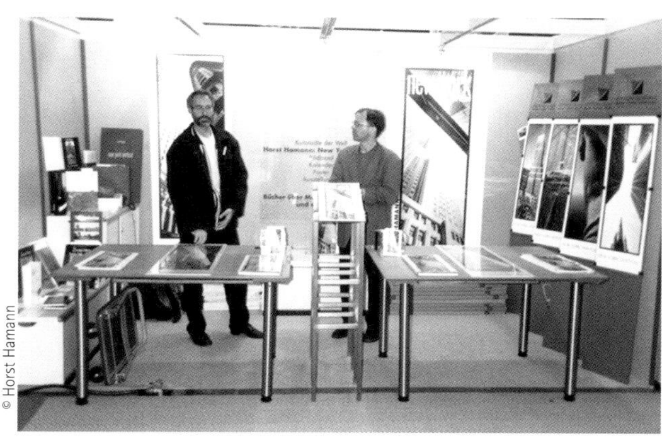

Publisher Bernhard Wipfler and Wolfgang Roth
International Book Fair Frankfurt

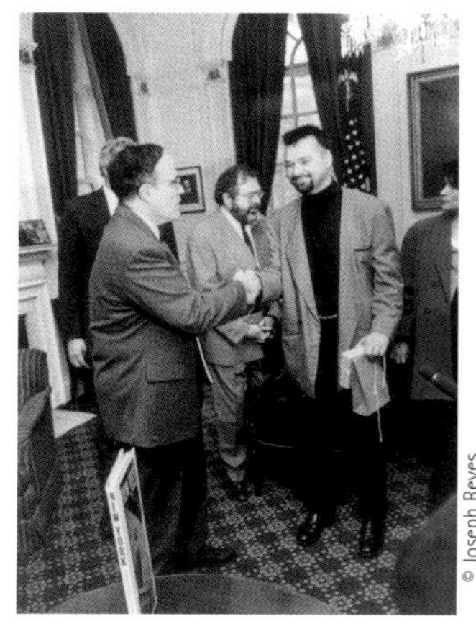

Mayor Rudolph Giuliani honors Horst Hamann with the "Seal of New York for his body New York Vertical"
City Hall, New York

1996

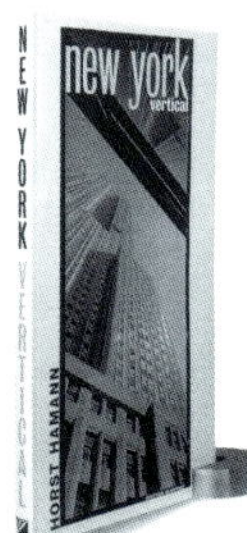

First German Edition of New York Vertical
(66 Duotone Photographs)

1996

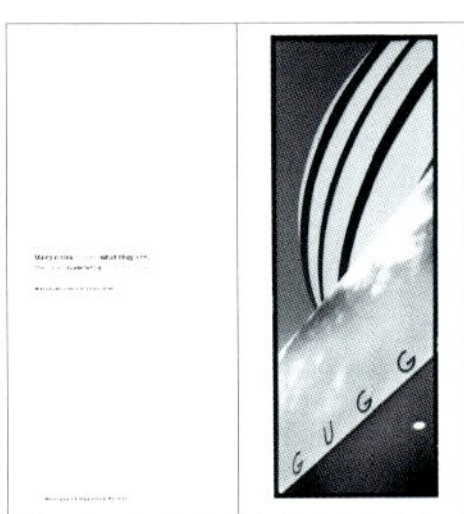

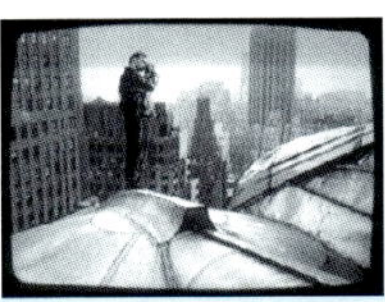

TV Documentary
Horst Hamann(NY)
SDR 3 Stuttgart

1997

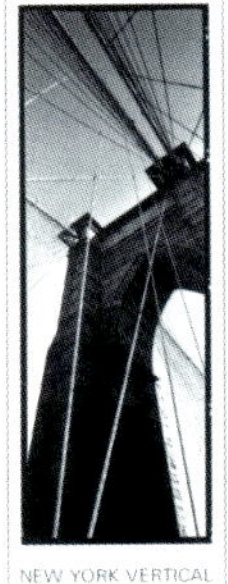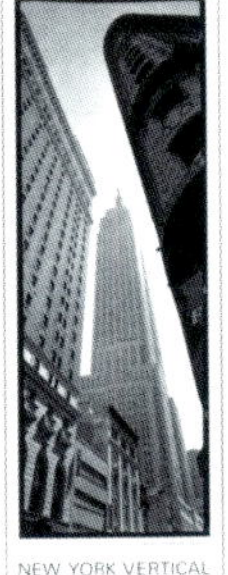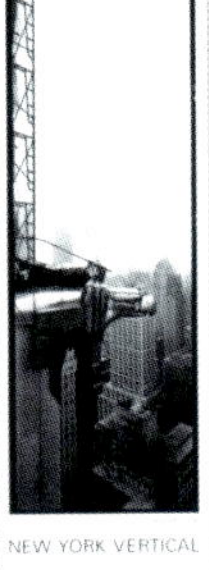

Poster Series , New York Vertical

1998–1999

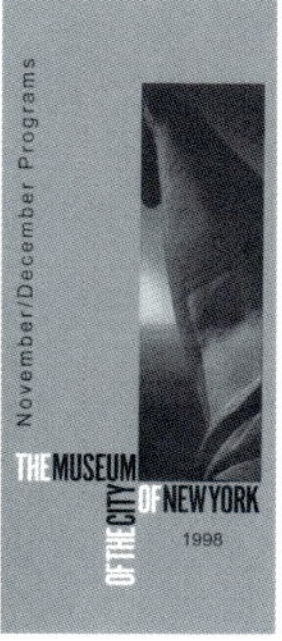

1998–1999

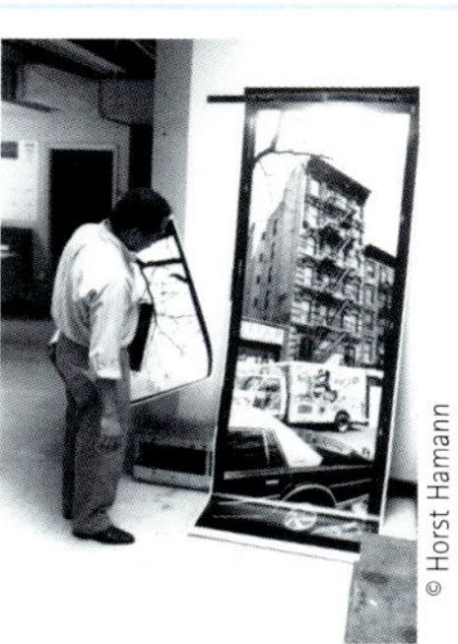

Lloyd Peterson, Modernage, NY
Producing large fromat exhibition prints
New York

© Horst Hamann

1998

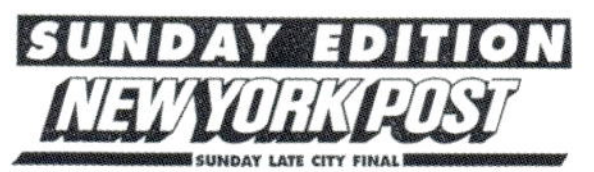

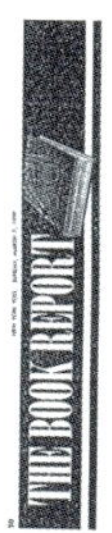

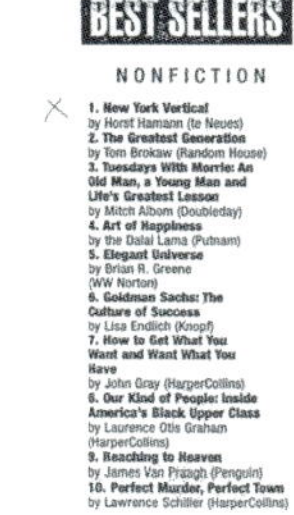

BEST SELLERS

NONFICTION

1. **New York Vertical**
by Horst Hamann (te Neues)
2. **The Greatest Generation**
by Tom Brokaw (Random House)
3. **Tuesdays With Morrie: An Old Man, a Young Man and Life's Greatest Lesson**
by Mitch Albom (Doubleday)
4. **Art of Happiness**
by the Dalai Lama (Putnam)
5. **Elegant Universe**
by Brian R. Greene (WW Norton)
6. **Goldman Sachs: The Culture of Success**
by Lisa Endlich (Knopf)
7. **How to Get What You Want and Want What You Have**
by John Gray (HarperCollins)
8. **Our Kind of People: Inside America's Black Upper Class**
by Laurence Otis Graham (HarperCollins)
9. **Reaching to Heaven**
by James Van Praagh (Penguin)
10. **Perfect Murder, Perfect Town**
by Lawrence Schiller (HarperCollins)

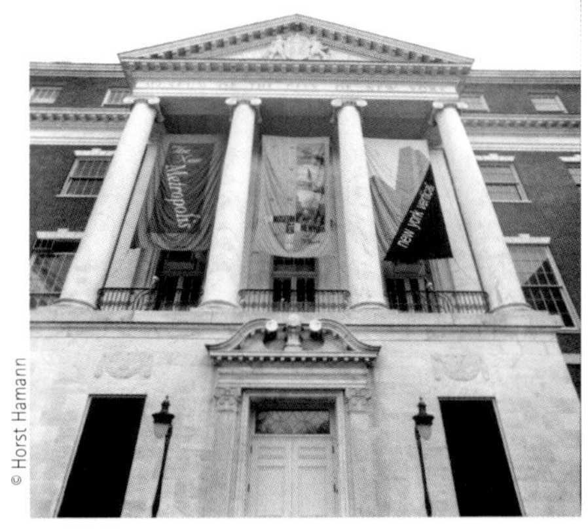

*Exhibition New York Vertical at
The Museum of the City of New York
November 1998 - May 1999*
New York

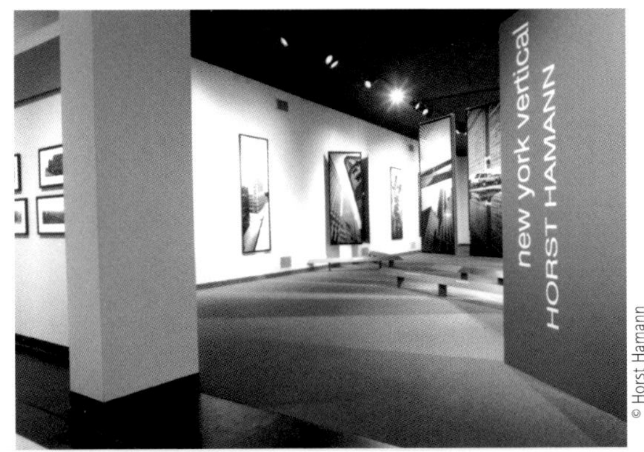

*Installation of thirty-five,
8 feet high silver gelatin prints*
New York

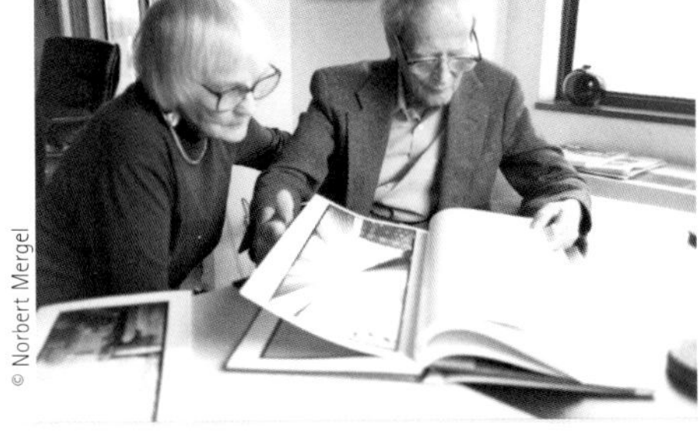

Wysse and Andreas Feininger
New York

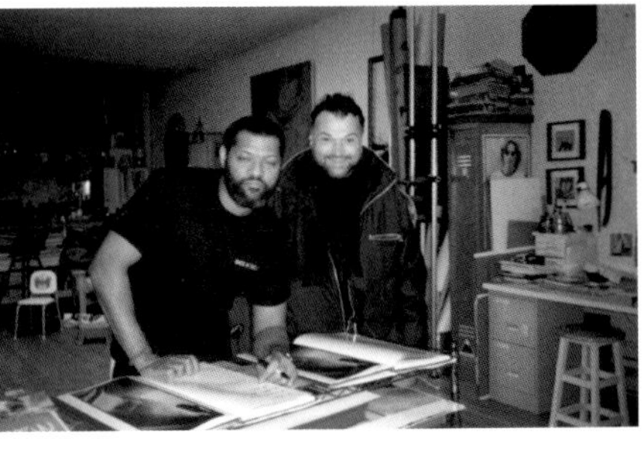

*Horst Hamann
with Laurence Fishburn*
Tribeca, New York

1999

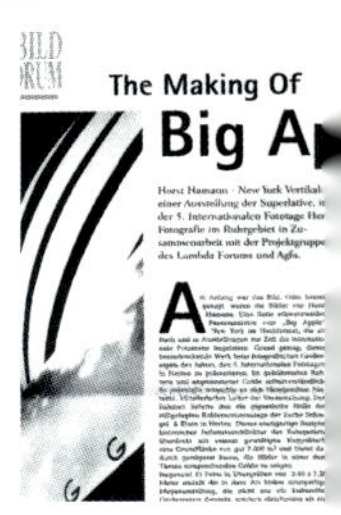

1999

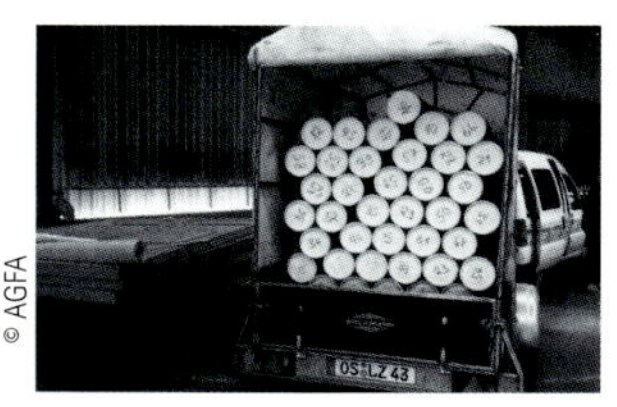

1999

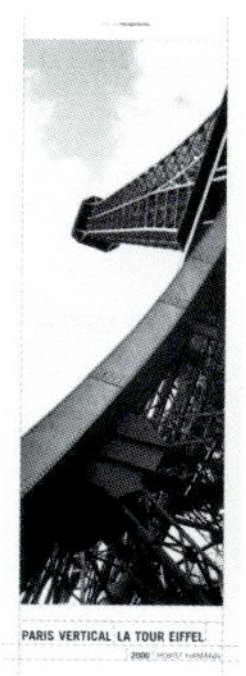
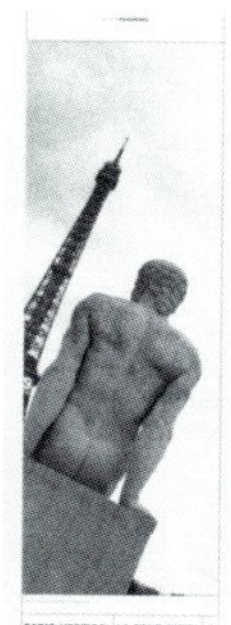
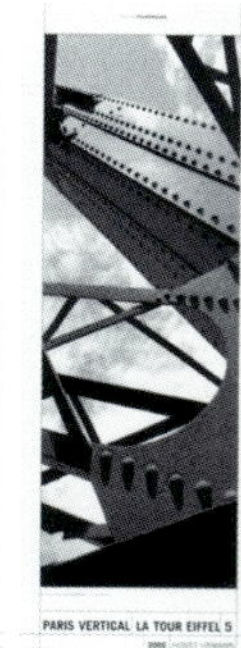

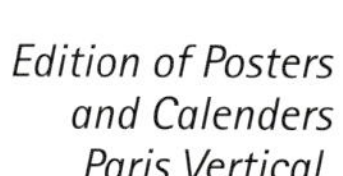

*Edition of Posters
and Calenders
Paris Vertical.*

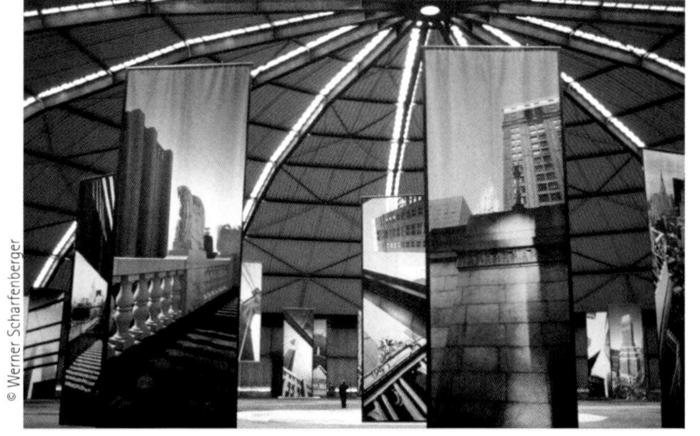

New York Vertical Installation of
forty-five 24 feet high digital prints
in a former 70,000 sq. foot
industrial dome.
Internationale Fototage Herten

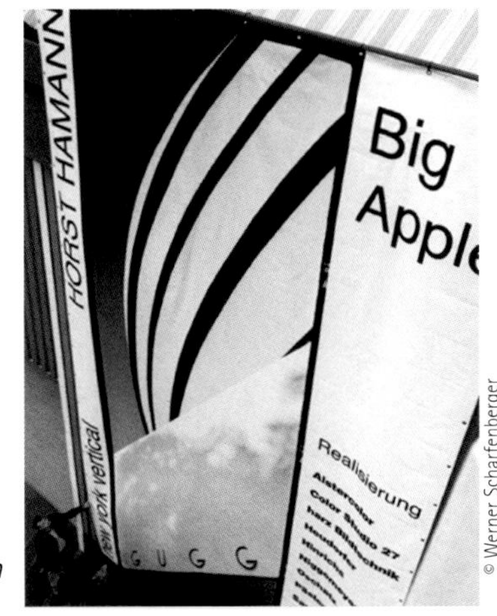

Internationale Fototage Herten

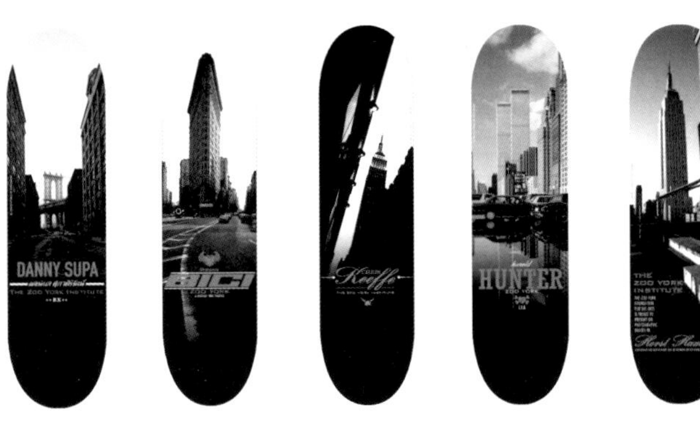

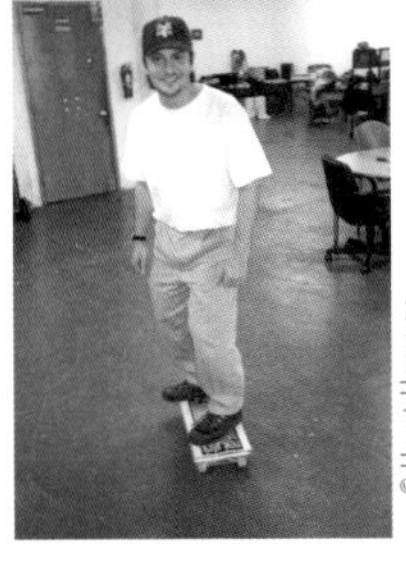

Top: Special Vertical
Skateboard Edition.
Published by Zoo York
Bottom: Adam Schatz
Zoo York, New York

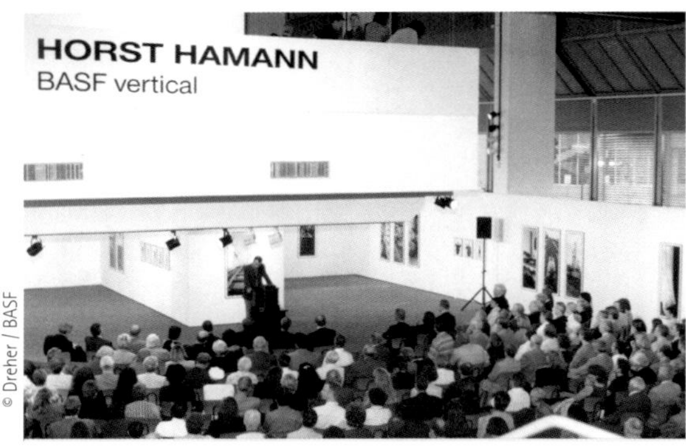

BASF Vertical – Faces of a Company.
Wilhelm-Hack-Museum,
Ludwigshafen / Rh.

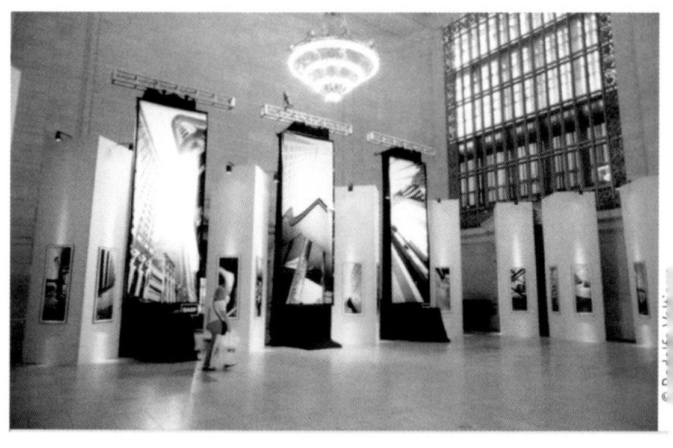

*Installation of 80 Verticals of New York
and BASF Industrials at Vanderbilt Hall*
Grand Central Terminal,
New York

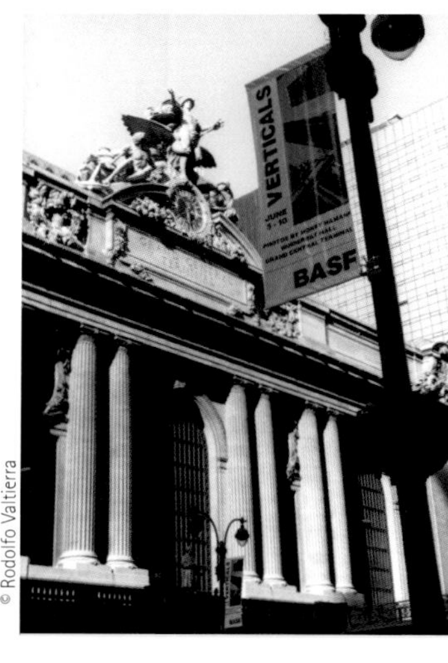

Verticals
Grand Central Terminal, New York

1999

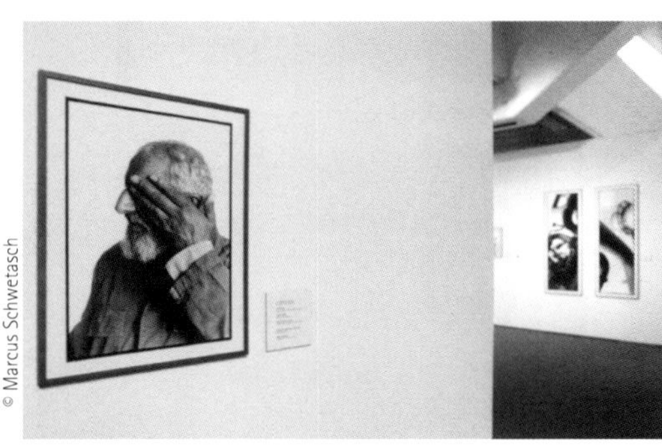

BASF Vertical – Faces of a Company.
148 Verticals and Portraits
Wilhelm-Hack-Museum,
Ludwigshafen / Rh.

2000

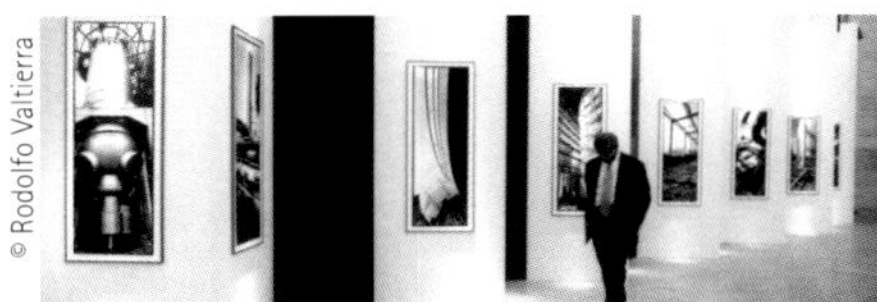

2000

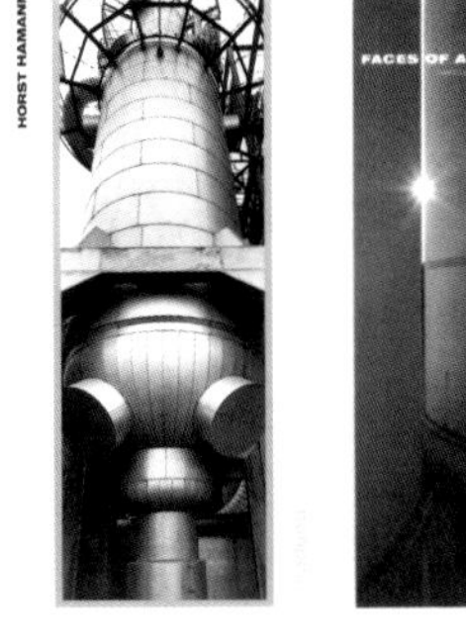
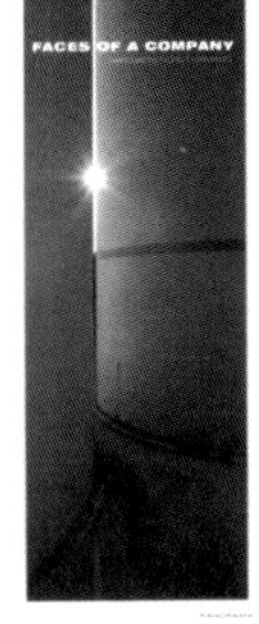

Faces of a Company
Book publication containing 72
industrial verticals and 106 portraits.

1981 *Cars and Stripes*
Fotografische Sammlung Bongartz, Krefeld

1981 *Living in Ameri-Car*
Triad Gallery, Portland, Maine

1984 *Bilder einer Ausstellung*
Künstlerhaus am Karlsplatz, Vienna

1984 *This is not America*
Bonner Kunstwoche, Künstlerzelt, Bonn

1985 *Künstlerportraits*
Kunsthaus Hamburg, Hamburg

1986 *Konfrontationen*
Ernst Museum, Budapest

1996 *New York Vertical*
Photokina, Cologne

1999 *New York Vertical*
Museum of the City of New York, New York

1999 *New York Vertical*
Internationale Fototage Herten

1999 *Neue Wege in der Industriefotografie*
Wilhelm-Hack-Museum, Ludwigshafen

1999 *New York Vertical*
Galerie Kasten, Mannheim

2000 *Verticals*
Vanderbilt Hall, Grand Central Terminal, New York

2001 *Vertical View, 1991-2001*
Center for Maine Contemporary Arts, Rockport, Maine

2002 *Vertical Game*
Galerie Beckers, Frankfurt

1985 *Glaube, Liebe, Hoffnung*
Künstlerverband Bucharest, Bucharest

1987 *Zeitraum*
Raum für fotografische Ansichten, Krefeld

1990 *Blau-Farbe der Ferne*
Kunstverein, Heidelberg

1991 *Botticelli meets Beuys*
Centre Culturel, Montpellier

1993 *Absolut Manhattan*
Nikon House, New York

1997 *New York Vertical*
Kunst-und Ausstellungshalle der
Bundesrepublik Deutschland, Bonn

1997 *New York Vertical*
Haus der Architekten, Stuttgart

1997 *New York, New York*
Arke Galerie, Dortmund

1998 *New York Vertical*
Nikon Image House, Zurich

2000 *Miniature*
Centre d'Art Microscopique, Paris

2001 *City*
Brooke Alexander Gallery, New York

2002 *Contrasts*
National Arts Club, New York

1981 *Augenscheinliches aus den USA*
Wilhelm-Hack-Museum, Ludwigshafen; Tonbilder

1981 *Augenscheinliches aus den USA*
Kunstverein Heidelberg; Tonbilder

1983 *Konfrontationen - Künstlerportraits*
Rathaushalle, Munich; Tonbilder

1983 *Farbwanderungen*
Galerie der Künstler, Munich; Tonbilder

1989 *Sinnfonie für Amphitrite*
Friedrichsplatz, Mannheim
Open air Drama on the occasion of the 100th
birthday of the Water Tower. Production for 100
dancers, lasers, pyro. 12,000 square feet slide
projection onto façade of the landmark building.
Multimedia: Stage Design, Direction

1991   *Licht Theater I*
        Internationales Congress Centrum, Hamburg
        Stage production with four dancers from
        four continents. Projection, movable screens
        Multimedia: Stage Design Direction

1994   *Images without Images*
        Electronic Nuyorican Poets Cafe,
        New York - Los Angeles - San Francisco
        Text & Camera

1995   *Urban Aid*
        Madison Square Garden, New York
        Anti - AIDS short film: They didn't know...
        Camera

1996   *Runaway*
        Janet Jackson
        Music Video (Dir. Marcus Nispel), New York
        Photography

1998   *Everything is Everything*
        Lauryn Hill
        Music Video (Dir. Sanji), New York
        Photography

2000   *Zeitpunkt 2000*
        Global Millennium project
        Invitation for 144 photographers around the world
        to shoot four identical subjects at
        simultaneous moments
        Web Project

1981   *Marx, M.*
        Eine individuelle Optik von Amerika
        in Die Rheinpfalz,Ludwigshafen/Rh. 12/81

1983   *Prestele, Charly*
        Ein Experiment der Gemeinschaft
        in Mannheimer Morgen, 5/83

1983   *Dressler, Otto*
        Tonbilder und Malerei
        in Kulturpolitik, Bonn 2/83

1983   *Wiedemann, Christoph*
        Konfrontationen und Tonbilder
        in Süddeutsche Zeitung, Munich 5/83

1985   *Bee, Andreas*
        Die Unvordenklichkeit des
        Bildes bei Horst Hamann
        in Katalog 3.2.1. Raum auf Zeit, Mannheim 1985

1988   *Weitenkopf, Diana*
        Die subjektive Sicht durchs Objektiv
        in Mannheimer Stadtillustrierte, Mannheim 1988

1988   *Kiausch, Usch*
        Zeitraum, Gleichzeitig - Gleichgültig ?
        in Communale, Heidelberg 1988

1994   *Hughes, Holly Stuart*
        Horst Hamann loves New York
        in Photo District News, New York 4/94

1995   *Klant, Michael*
        Künstler bei der Arbeit von Fotografen gesehen
        in Cantz Verlag, Ostfildern-Ruit 1995

1996   *Witte, Peter*
        Ein Buch und sein Autor
        in Photopresse, Münden 42/96

1996   *Wolf, Stephan*
        Mit der Kamera in schwindelnder Höhe
        in Mannheimer Morgen 11/96

1996   *Klünder, Irene*
        Wenn das Bauwerk das Format bestimmt
        in Börsenblatt, Frankfurt/Main 57/96

1996   *Hess, Hans-Eberhard*
        New York Vertical
        in Photo Technik International, Munich 9/96

1996   *Langer, Freddy*
        So hoch - Horst Hamann fotografiert New York
        in Frankfurter Allgemeine Zeitung 227/96

1996   *Forti, Guilio*
        New York Vertical
        in Fotografia Reflex, Milano 200/96

1996   *Langen, Andreas*
        New York vertikal - die Wolkenkratzer -
        City im Hochformat
        in Stuttgarter Zeitung 50/96

1996   *New York Vertical*
        in Sonderheft kursiv, Bauwelt, Berlin 28/96

1997	*Tomes for the Holiday* in Conde Nasté Traveler, New York 12/97
1997	*Jst* Ganz hoch hinaus in Hannoverische Allgemeine Zeitung, 11/97
1997	*New York Vertical* in Photomarket, New York 9/97
1997	*Hughes, Holly Stuart* Photo Design Award - Horst Hamann New York Vertical in Photo District News, New York 3/97
1997	*Willemsen, Roger* New York Vertical in Vogue, Munich 1/97
1997	*Langen, Andreas* New York Vertical in Die Woche, Hamburg 3/97
1997	*Drommert, Jürgen* New York Vertical in New York, Architektur & Wohnen, spezial 2, Hamburg 1997
1997	*Horst Hamann: New York Vertical* Europäischer Architekturfotografie Preis in Deutsche Bauzeitung, Stuttgart 5/97
1997	*New York Vertical* in High Quality, Munich 1/97
1997	*Weisman, Melissa A.* Photographer Horst Hamann shoots for the top in Hampton Country Magazine, South Hampton 9/97
1997	*Telford, Anne* New York Vertical in Communication Arts, Palo Alto CA 9/97
1997	*Look this way New York* in Daily News, New York 12/97
1997	*New York Vertical* in Forbes Magazine, New York 12/97
1997	*Adams, Cindy* New York Vertical Book Report in New York Post, New York 12/97
1998	*Klarwein-Milinaire, Serafine* Horst Hamann In Night Magazine, New York 1/98
1998	*Augenschmaus* in Die Zeit, Hamburg 52/98
1998	*Newill, Eric* Best Books in Ocean Drive Magazine, Miami 1/98
1998	*MacNeille, Suzanne* Head for Heights in New York Times, New York 3/98
1998	*Guide to really big books* in The Photograph Colector, Langhorn PA 12/98
1998	*Pedersen, Anke* Senkrechtstarter in Wirtschaftswoche, Düsseldorf 51/98
1999	*Guttmann, Katja* Horst Hamann / Portfolio in Photographie 7-8/99 und 9/99
1999	*Lorenz, Dieter* Panorama verkehrt in MFM Fototechnik - Kultur, Ludwigsburg 7/99
1999	*Wappler, Dietrich* Die Fabrik in voller Grösse in Die Rheinpfalz, Ludwigshafen/Rhein 216/99
1999	*Heybrock, Christel* Zwangloses Wechselspiel von Mensch und Mythos in Mannheimer Morgen, Mannheim 215/99
1999	*Berlinghof, Harald* Neue Wege in der Industriefotografie in Rhein-Neckar-Zeitung, Heidelberg 9/99
1999	*Best Seller List #1: Non-fiction* Horst Hamann, New York Vertical in New York Post, New York 3/99
1999	*Horst Hamann - Americana* Communication Arts in Photography Annual 40, Palo Alto 8/99
1999	*Horst Hamann - New York Vertical* in Profi Foto, Düsseldorf 9/99

1999   *Zollner, Manfred*
        Horst Hamann - Paris Vertical, Portfolio
        in Foto Magazin, Munich 11/99

1999   *Portrait Horst Hamann*
        in Stern, Hamburg 10/99

1999   *G.I.*
        Internationale Fototage in Herten
        in Frankfurter Allgemeine Zeitung,
        Frankfurt 10/99

1999   *Big Apple im Ruhrgebiet*
        in Schwarzweiss 22, Frankfurt 10-11/99

1999   *Hepä*
        Die Krönung des bisherigen Fotofestivals
        in Foto Contact, Herten 12/99

1999   *Wagner, Thorsten*
        New York Vertical von Horst Hamann in
        der Hertener Rundhalle setzt Maßstäbe
        in Hertener Allgemeine, Herten 7/99

1999   *New York Vertical*
        in Large Format, Bochum 5/99

1999   *New York Vertical*
        in Foto Wirtschaft, Munich 8/99

1999   *aho*
        Das XL Foto Spektakel
        in Photo Technik International, Munich 6/99

1999   *G.U.*
        Internationale Fototage Herten -
        Hamann's Inszenierung
        in Photo Presse, Hann. Münden 41/99

1999   *Schelhorn, Tina*
        The Making of Big Apple
        in Das Bild Forum, Herten 7/99

1999   *Muschamp, Herbert*
        Steel Dreams That the Eye Can Cherish
        in New York Times, New York 1/99

2000   *APO*
        You can hold this sideways, too - NY Vertical
        in Die Welt - Atlantic Daily,
        Berlin - London - New York 4/00

2000   *Kleinschmidt, Klaus*
        Bizz-Edition, Horst Hamann
        in Bizz, Köln 2/00

2000   *Jackson, Sarah*
        Reach for the Sky
        in Amateur Photographer, London 4/00

2000   *Trende, Klaus*
        Ansichten von der Megamaschine
        in Lausitzer Rundschau - Kultur, Lausitz 12/00

2000   *Atherton, Nigel*
        Best pictures of the year
        in Amateur Photographer -
        Special Collectors Issue, London 12/00

2001   *Isaacson, Philip*
        A camera turned on end
        in Maine Sunday Telegram, Portland 5/01

2001   *Saebisch, Babette*
        Der Waghalsige unter den Fotografen
        in Der Frankfurter, Frankfurt 3-4/01

2001   *The hottest People, Places and Things on the planet*
        in Gear Magazine, New York 1/01

2001   *Graeber, Laurel*
        Attractions - Flatiron Building
        in New York Times, New York 2/01

1989   *SDR 3, Süddeutscher Rundfunk TV*
        Sinnfonie für Amphitrite
        in Abendschau, Stuttgart 1989

1995   *SDR 3, Süddeutscher Rundfunk TV*
        Klünder, Irene
        Portrait; Horst Hamann über New York
        in Landesschau, Stuttgart 1995

1996   *WDR 3, Westdeutscher Rundfunk, Radio*
        Hoven, Herbert
        NY Vertical - ein Bildband von Horst Hamann
        in Mosaik, Cologne 1996

1997   *ARD, Süddeutscher Rundfunk TV*
        Krupok, Isolde
        Horst Hamann in New York
        in Mensch, Leute!, Stuttgart 1997

1997 *ARTE - TV*
Pütz, Günter
Horst Hamann und seine vertikale Sichtweise
in Metropolis, Strasbourg 1997

1998 *Bloomberg Radio*
Lee, Jean
Horst Hamann's Verticals -
Museum of the City of New York
in Interview New York 1998

1998 *ZDF, Zweites Deutsches Fernsehen TV*
Hess, Jutta
New York im Hochformat -
die Fotos von Horst Hamann
in Aspekte, Mainz 1998

1998 *SWF 1, Südwestfunk Radio*
Naumer, Andreas
Studiogast Horst Hamann
in So Wars - New York Special, Stuttgart 1998

1998 *SWF, Südwestfunk TV*
Buettner, Tilmann
Im Schatten der Wall Street
in USA, Baden-Baden 1998

1998 *VIVA - TV*
Studiogast
Horst Hamann
in Amica-TV, Cologne 1998

1998 *WNBC - TV*
Taylor, Felicia
Horst Hamann at the
Museum of the City of New York
in Sunday Today in New York, New York 1998

1999 *RNF - TV*
Siegelmann, Bert
Studiogast Horst Hamann
in Profil, Mannheim 1999

1999 *SWR, Südwestrundfunk TV*
Kilwink, Isa
Der Senkrechtstarter
in Nahaufnahme, SWR, Mainz 1999

1999 *BBC - TV*
Potter, Elisabeth
New York Vertical
at the Museum of the City of New York
in BBC News, New York - London 1999

1999 *PBS - TV*
Deroy, Jaimee
Vertical Photographs at
the Museum of the City of New York
in City Arts, New York 1999

1999 *RNF - TV*
Boehm, Matthias
Horst Hamann - Faces of a Company
in Landesschau, Ludwigshafen 1999

1999 *ARTE - TV*
Burchardt, Melanie
Big Apple bei den Fototagen in Herten
in Tracks, Strasbourg 1999

1999 *SWR 3, Südwestrundfunk Radio*
Ries, Michael
Studiogast Horst Hamann
in Leute, Stuttgart 1999

1999 *SWR, Südwestrundfunk TV*
Hattensen, Maja
Neue Wege in der Industriefotografie
in Kulturreport, Mainz 1999

1999 *SWR, Südwestrundfunk TV*
Studiogast Horst Hamann
in Kultur Café, Mainz 1999

1999 *HR 3, Hessischer Rundfunk TV*
Soliman, Tina
Mr. Vertical
in Moderne Menschen, Frankfurt 1999

Agfa Gevaert Collection, Leverkusen

Fotografische Sammlung Bongartz, Krefeld

Museum of the City of New York, New York

Saatchi Collection, London

Portland Museum of Art, Portland

Goldman Sachs Collection, New York

1998	*The Panorama Seen Vertical* The Museum of the City of New York, New York
1999	*The Panorama Seen Vertical* The Camera Club of New York, New York
1999	*Vertical View* Fotoforum Herten, Int. Fototage, Herten
2000	*The Urban Landscape* International Center of Photography, New York
2001	*The Urban Landscape* International Center of Photography, New York
2001	*Vertical View* Center for Maine Contemporary Art, Rockport

1985	*Mannheim - Einblicke in eine Stadt* Südwestdeutsche Verlagsanstalt, Mannheim 1985
1988	*Zeitraum Gleichzeitig - Gleichgültig?* Edition Quadrat, Mannheim 1988
1991	*Jochen Sendler - Porträt eines Bildhauers* Edition Hierling, Munich 1991
1992	*Absolut Manhattan* N.Y. State of Mind Publishing, New York 1992
1994	*Look* N.Y. State of Mind Publishing, New York 1994
1996	*New York Vertical* Edition Quadrat, Mannheim 1996
1999	*Faces of a Company* Edition Panorama, Mannheim 1999
2001	*N.Y. Lounge* CD, Blue Flame Records, Stuttgart 2001
2001	*Horst Hamann New York* Edition Panorama, Mannheim 2001
2001	*Vertical View* Edition Panorama, Mannheim 2001

1996	*Kodak Photo Book Award* New York Vertical
1996	*Stiftung Buchkunst, Most Beautiful Books* New York Vertical
1997	*DB Architekturbild* New York Vertical
1997	*Photo Design Gold Award: poster* New York Vertical
1997	*Kodak Photo Calendar Award* New York Vertical
1997	*Stuttgart Calendar Show Award* New York Vertical
1998	*Photo Design Gold Award: calendar* New York Vertical
1998	*Photo Design Gold Award: book* New York Vertical
1999	*Kodak Photo Calendar Award* Americana
1999	*Photo Design Gold Award* Americana
1999	*Stuttgart Calendar Show Award* Americana
1999	*Communcation Arts Award* Americana
2000	*Photo Design Gold Award* Paris Vertical
2000	*Photo Design Silver Award* Faces of A Company

1958	*Born in Mannheim, Germany.* He lives with his wife and two sons in New York and Maine.

For My Parents

Marie, Maren, Paula, Maria Hamann, Johannes Hamann, Matthias & Stephanie Hamann, Heinrich Gröger, Bernhard Wipfler, Sebastian & Benjamin Wipfler, Wolle Roth, Irmgard Kuhn - Geisselhart, Hendrik te Neues, Michael Gray, Rachel Wixom, Harold Thieck, Marcus Herfort, Hr. Dahm, Sonja Bullaty, Angelo Lomeo, Andreas Bee, Serafine Klarwein - Milinaire, Werner Bochmann, Karl-Heinz Rohrmann, Ismael Dogan, Sabine E. Mader, Jochen Rohner, Michael Gregoire, Robert & Ann Brochu, Hansjoachim Nierentz, Karin Weber - Andreas, Tina Schelhorn, Kenneth & Richard Troiano, Joseph Smith, JJ. Straub, Vi Nguyen, Tilo Kaiser, Jutta Hess, Udo van Kampen, Susanne Lingemann, Robert Polecek, Norbert Mergel, Ludwig Linden, Thomas Breuer, Cornelia Franz, Leo Strohm, Suzanne Nicholas, Veronique Nguyen, Paul Pagk, Danja Gazzara, Nora Küppers, Andrea Leminske, Dorian Romer, Werner Schwarzer, Sarah Tittle, Jack Montgomery, Roger & Ana Conover, Bruce Brown, Jo Weinberg, Ron Paragallo, Wulf & Irene Liebau, Anita Beckers, Ilona Ortner, Friedemann Leinert, Caterine Milinaire, Nadia & Pierre Valla, Friedrich Kasten, Howard Greenberg, Marla Hamburg - Kennedy, Michael Hoppen, Michelle Dennison, Tilman Buettner, Gerhard Vormwald, Mark Robinow, Volker Skierka, Roberto Costa, Nurit, Isa Kilwink, Dorien Romer, Deirdree Murphy, Lutz Bernstein, Marcus Nispel, Kevin Breslin, Steffi Probst, Mark & Aimee Bessire, Matthias Hensel, Lothar Meinzer, Felix Gress, Werner Scharfenberger, Diana Weitenkopf, Liane Kranhold, Tina Soliman, Torsten Lapp, Cecile zu Hohenlohe, Cyril de Commarque, Gero Ulmrich, Sabine Schmitt, Jochen Sendler, Andrea Dörr, Susanne Rüde, Stephen Hulburt, Kate Feindel, Prita Meier, C.M. Landegger, Babette Grospiron, Fam. Dominique Preaud, Steh & Willi, Petra Loewen, Dennis & Diane Griggs, Leon Kouyoumijian, David Rowland, Svetlana Petroff, Thomas Zeumer, Klaus Sauer, David Mishken, Judy & Joe, Marcus Schwetasch, Gerd & Linde Schwetasch, Bob Horn, Sanji, Timothy Whelan, Andrea Hambuechen, Kate Goodspeed, Margaret Donovan, Ken Hansen, Zoo York: Adam Schatz, Eli Morgan Gesner, Rodney Smith, Dave, Jefferson Pang, Dany Supa, Anthony Correa, Quim Cardona, Alice Müller.

Special Thanks to Nielsen & Bainbridge.

Thanks

First Edition 2001

© 2001 EDITION PANORAMA, Germany and Horst Hamann

Published by EDITION PANORAMA, Germany
Published internationally by te Neues Publishing Group Kempen, London, New York, Paris, Toronto
© all Photographs by Horst Hamann except where indicated
The image of the Solomon R. Guggenheim Museum is a registered trademark
© 2001 Introduction by Andreas Bee
Editorial department United States: Limited Eyedition, Inc.
Marie Hamann, Sarah Tittle, Dominique Preaud
Editorial department Germany: EDITION PANORAMA
Wolfgang Roth, Tatjana Strasser
Translations: Jeremy Gaines, Renate Manceau, Pia Neumann
Art department: Limited Eyedition, Inc.
Horst Hamann, Michael Gregoire
Design: Michael Gregoire
Separations: Werner Bochmann, Scantronic
CTP: Fotosatz Hörn
Printing: Brausdruck GmbH, Heidelberg
Printed on Heidelberg Speedmaster
Printed on BVS-matt 150 g, Papierfabrik Scheufelen
Binding: Buchbinderei Fikentscher, Darmstadt
ISBN: 3-89823-162-3 (german edition)
ISBN: 3-8238-5562-X (international edition)
All rights reserved
Printed in Germany
No part of this book may be reproduced in any form or by any electronic or mechanical means
without prior written permission from the original publisher EDITION PANORAMA, Germany

A Production by EDITION**PANORAMA** Germany · Publisher Bernhard Wipfler

www.horsthamann.com
www.editionpanorama.de
www.teneues.com
www.limitedeyedition.com